Cambridge Ele

Elements in Archaeological Perspec...
Technologies
edited by
A. Mark Pollard
University of Oxford
Chris Gosden
University of Oxford

AN ARCHAEOLOGICAL PERSPECTIVE ON THE HISTORY OF TECHNOLOGY

A. Mark Pollard
University of Oxford
Chris Gosden
University of Oxford

CAMBRIDGE
UNIVERSITY PRESS

CAMBRIDGE
UNIVERSITY PRESS

Shaftesbury Road, Cambridge CB2 8EA, United Kingdom

One Liberty Plaza, 20th Floor, New York, NY 10006, USA

477 Williamstown Road, Port Melbourne, VIC 3207, Australia

314–321, 3rd Floor, Plot 3, Splendor Forum, Jasola District Centre,
New Delhi – 110025, India

103 Penang Road, #05–06/07, Visioncrest Commercial, Singapore 238467

Cambridge University Press is part of Cambridge University Press & Assessment,
a department of the University of Cambridge.

We share the University's mission to contribute to society through the pursuit of
education, learning and research at the highest international levels of excellence.

www.cambridge.org
Information on this title: www.cambridge.org/9781009184212

DOI: 10.1017/9781009184205

First published 2023

A catalogue record for this publication is available from the British Library.

ISBN 978-1-009-18421-2 Paperback
ISSN 2632-7031 (online)
ISSN 2632-7023 (print)

An Archaeological Perspective on the History of Technology

Elements in Archaeological Perspectives on Materials and Technologies

DOI: 10.1017/9781009184205
First published online: February 2023

A. Mark Pollard
University of Oxford

Chris Gosden
University of Oxford

Author for correspondence: A. Mark Pollard, Mark.pollard@arch.ox.ac.uk

Abstract: This volume represents an introduction to a new worldwide attempt to review the history of technology, which is one of the few since the pioneering publications of the 1960s. It takes an explicit archaeological focus to the study of the history of technology and adopts a more explicit socially embedded view of technology than has commonly been the case in mainstream histories of technology. In doing so, it attempts to introduce a more radical element to explanations of technological change, involving magic, alchemy, animism – in other words, attempting to consider technological change in terms of the 'world view' of those involved in such change rather than from an exclusively Western scientific perspective.

Keywords: technology, history, archaeology, cognition, perception

ISBNs: 9781009184212 (PB), 9781009184205 (OC)
ISSNs: 2632-7031 (online), 2632-7023 (print)

Contents

After the First Emperor of the Qin had united the world and proclaimed himself emperor, someone advised him, saying, 'the Yellow Emperor ruled by the power of the element earth, therefore a yellow dragon and a great earthworm appeared in this time. The Xia dynasty ruled by the power of wood, and so a green dragon came to rest in its court and the grasses and trees grew luxuriantly. The Shang dynasty ruled by metal (金), and silver (銀) flowed out of the mountains. The Zhou ruled by fire, and therefore it was given a sign in the form of a red bird. Now the Qin has replaced the Zhou, and the era of the power of water has come'.

Watson (1961)

Introduction

This is the first volume in a series devoted to creating new archaeological perspectives on the history of technology, to be published by Cambridge Elements. The aim of this volume is essentially to set the scene for the rest of the series – to explain *why* we think a new perspective is required, and what we think is *new* about the approach to be followed. To capture the basic intention of the series in a simple sentence, it would be to say that '*on a worldwide basis, and from the earliest human use of tools, we are interested in how things were done, why they were done that way, and how that knowledge was communicated'*. These objectives would, of course, be shared by most if not all histories of technology. The other aspect of the series, which is perhaps less ubiquitous, is to explore the view that technology represents a socially embedded set of activities, sustained by the transmission of relevant bodies of knowledge and practices. So, at the highest level, the aim of this volume, and of the series as a whole, includes:

1. to integrate recent technological and archaeological work with newer theoretical perspectives (including ideas of materiality, and explicitly avoiding the concept of 'progress');
2. more specifically to explore the idea of material engagement: that both traditions and novelty emerge from a partnership between the capacities of human bodies and the possibilities offered by various materials;
3. to make connections between regions and across time;
4. to amplify voices or cultures that have previously been marginalized in most narratives on technology; and,
5. to query the evidence of material remains in new ways (including ways that take advantage of massively increased computing power and large data sets, etc.).

In effect, the aim of this series is to explore the boundaries between knowledge, belief, motivation, and practice in the context of technological processes. One of the most significant changes in the way in which archaeologists have approached technological studies of the material record in recent years has been the adoption of the *chaîne opératoire* (Leroi-Gourhan, 1964, 1965; Schlanger, 1994; Sillar and Tite, 2000). At one level, this involves documenting the technological choices made during a manufacturing process, such as the selection of materials and techniques made by a potter, as far as can be reconstructed from a study of the object and whatever other material remains are available. In practice, however, the approach is designed to help us understand, through an analysis of these choices, the intentions in the mind of the potter at the time of manufacture, be they conscious choices or simply a consequence of learnt practice and behaviour. As such, it offers one way of addressing some of the difficult questions about *intentionality* outlined in this volume.

The approach taken will be heavily influenced by archaeological evidence, including evidence from the technical studies of the objects and their manufacturing debris, but also by ethnographic data, and obviously drawing on literary sources when they are available. It will also be characterized by efforts to break down traditional material-based barriers, both in terms of thinking about cross-craft interactions, but also in recognizing the mutual dependence between different materials (McGovern, 1989; Brysbaert, 2007, 2011). When discussing material culture, the use of traditional material-based categories (e.g., 'ceramic', 'metal', 'glass') is almost inevitable in large scale studies – it recognizes the relative homogeneity of properties and processes within each category, and also the obvious differences between categories. The technologies and properties of metal are clearly different in many respects from those of, say, ceramics. The use of these categories also provides a convenient boundary to the scope of any particular discussion. Nevertheless, it clearly downplays the complexity of the real world, and in particular the necessary interplay between different materials in the execution of many technologies. A simple example would be the need for the creation of a mould from clay or stone prior to the casting of metal. Arguably, therefore, we cannot discuss the technology of metal casting without also considering the associated technologies of ceramic materials or stone carving. Indeed, it is hard to think about a manufacturing technology for a particular material which does not require some consideration of the use of other materials – including, of course, the skills of the human body. Although requiring a conscious effort, such intersections can often be recognized and discussed, and will lead towards a better understanding of the complexity and entanglement of the material and human worlds.

The scope of the series – in terms of time, space, and concepts – is, admittedly, massive. One of the great challenges of undertaking such an enterprise is to come up with a series volume structure which reflects the overall ambition, and it is here that we have to admit to compromise. The systematic delivery of knowledge requires segmentation into recognizable units capable of being used as stand-alone contributions, whilst still combining to provide a more holistic whole.

After much consideration, and somewhat reluctantly, we have decided to structure the series thematically, so there will be volumes on topics such as communication technologies, lithics, pigments, building technologies, textiles, ceramics, glass, agriculture, food, metals, transport, military technologies, synthetic chemistry and technologies of power. Within this structure, however, we aim to cover all aspects of material culture including transport, housing, food procurement and preparation, decorative arts, weapons, and so forth.

We propose to encompass all human society, on a worldwide basis, from the technological achievements of early hominins, through to an end date which is admittedly difficult to define precisely. The imposition of an end date is partly necessitated by the approach taken – archaeological and ethnographical approaches to the material record are partial sources of evidence once we enter the early modern world. Perhaps more critical, however, is the concept that the economic and social structure of the world changed with the arrival of what is called in the West the 'Industrial Revolution'. Although many would see this as a false boundary, and it is not directly relevant to large parts of the world, it nevertheless very broadly marked the transition from the traditional sources of power – human and animal muscle, alongside harnessed fire, wind and water – to the domination by mechanical sources of power, which eventually changed the whole relationship between humans and nature in many parts of the world. Naturally, this 'power divide' occurred at different times in different places, but in Europe a convenient boundary would be around 1700 CE, representing a time after the end of the medieval period in Europe (*c.*1500 CE), but before the major impacts of steam power.

Because the aim of the series is to give a global perspective, the structure of the series cannot be rigidly chronological – indeed to construct these volumes in such a way would be to risk reinforcing problematic notions of unilinear technological and cultural development, which we wish to avoid. For example, the lithic technology of Aboriginal Australians, which represents a living trad-ition despite many centuries of colonial suppression, will be discussed in the same volume as prehistoric lithic technology. This is in no way intended to revive outdated and offensive concepts of 'primitive' cultures, so characteristic of nineteenth century colonial anthropology and evolutionary social theory. It is simply to recognize the reality of the continuity of tradition in some parts of the world, and perhaps also to underline the efficacy of earlier technological solu-tions in particular social and environmental contexts, rendering the idea of 'technological progress' an irrelevance. Such situations therefore provide an important contrast and benchmark by which to assess the perceived opportun-ities or necessities for those technological changes which did occur elsewhere.

As noted in the Introduction, the series will explicitly try to avoid explanations of technological change based solely on concepts of 'progress' or 'development', in which technology is seen as either the means or a consequence of the inevitable progression from a primitive state to the modern state of social and technological enlightenment. These concepts are very much associated with European colonial expansionism, and are neither helpful nor applicable to the longer and broader history of humankind – classic statements of progress powered by technological change being Childe's *Man Makes Himself* (1936) but are encoded into much of Processual Archaeology, finding a reprise in current work such as Ian Morris's *Why the West Rules (for Now)* (2010). They are often also linked to an earlier view of technology as representing and facilitating 'Man's increasing domination of Nature', which is a deep-rooted concept in Western thinking, probably arising from the biblical definition of man as the divinely appointed master of the Earth and all things within it (Leiss, 1972). Technology thus becomes the vehicle by which this domination is achieved, and the biblical authorization gives both legitimacy and the necessary driving force for technological development, and inherently undermines any alternative views.

Indeed, we argue that such notions of technology are anachronistic in the global context, in that the recognition that the concept of technology (in the sense of the use of tools to modify the world) may only have emerged in the last couple of millennia, and possibly only in the last five hundred years, as part of a Western view of the world that emphasises notions of cause and effect. As has often been pointed out, instead of cause and effect, many societies have embraced a different concept of participation with the world, developing ideas that we would label as animistic, magical, or religious (Descola, 2013). These offer a quite different starting point for the consideration of technology when compared to modern Western notions in which control over materials through understanding and measuring the physical principles by which they combine and change are the dominant features. Modern science and technology emerged from a complicated mix of alchemy, astrology, religion, and mysticism from the late medieval period onwards, but scientific approaches to the world are historically and culturally unusual in the broader context of human history.

Our histories of technology will therefore have two complementary strands. The first of these, relatively conventionally, will chart the history of techniques and materials, looking at the manner in which different materials have been incorporated into human life over several million years since the earliest tool use. The second strand will be more philosophical, probing the difficult questions of what human relations with the material world were, and, in understanding these, how far can we break out of the old antitheses between magic and science or ritual and technology (Gosden, 2020). The resulting contributions will explore the historical and cultural context of material culture, drawing on the latest theory in a range of relevant disciplines, but they will also apply empirically rich accounts incorporating the latest analytical results. We will look at the ways in which materials and techniques are invented and adopted, transmitted and transformed, in both practical and cultural contexts. Although we will of necessity engage with the growing complexity of technologies over time, we hope to do this in such a way as to question whether this apparent growth is largely a matter of scale, deriving from the increasing size and complexity of human societies, as implied in more linear explanations.

Setting the Scene

In 1900, a group of sponge divers, blown off course and diving for the first time near the coast of the small Greek island of Antikythera, saw a bronze hand laying on the seabed which proved to derive from an ancient wreck which we now know dates to around 80 BCE (De Sola Price, 1975). It is thought that this was a Roman ship perhaps travelling between Rhodes and Rome, carrying a cargo of fine objects including bronze and marble statues, as well as amphorae, luxury pottery and glass. An encrusted mass of bronze, initially ignored, has proved to be the most mysterious find of all and has excited great interest ever since, especially after scanning techniques revealed a mass of gear wheels within, connecting the circular movements of the front and back faces (Figure 1). Considerable investigation of this so-called Antikythera mechanism (e.g., Freeth et al., 2006, 2021; Evans et al., 2010; Jones, 2017; Efstathiou and Efstathiou, 2018), together with

Figure 1 The Antikythera mechanism. (National Archaeological Museum, Athens, licensed under CC BY 2.5)

detailed reconstructions, some by modern watch makers, has revealed the following possible interpretation, although this is not without its challenges. The mechanism was housed in a rectangular wooden frame over a front and back face with at least thirty-seven gear wheels in the interior, operated by turning a handle on the side of the device. The front shows an outer circle with the 365 days of the year according to the solar calendar derived from Egypt and an inner circle with the 12 signs of the zodiac. By moving the handle, the operator could show for each day of the year the exact position of the sun and moon, with a smaller sphere indicating the phases of the moon. An upper dial on the back of the device shows the so-called Metonic cycle (designating lunar months) based on the movements of the sun and moon over 19 years corresponding to 235 lunar months. A second spiral indicates eclipses of the sun and moon, so that the handle could be moved showing when the next eclipse would occur in the Saros cycle (a cycle of 223 lunar months useful for predicting eclipses of the sun and moon).

The gearing in the interior of the mechanism join the lunar and solar cycles, with the rising and setting of the moon happening on the same day once every nineteen solar years. Lying behind this mechanism is mathematics showing a grasp of the known universe, but also precision engineering to cast or cut the gear wheels of a correct size and number of teeth. Aspects of the universe were rendered mathematically in this device, but such knowledge is based on long observations of the heavens across the ancient world, and almost certainly also occurring prior to any written records. We do know that by the late first millennium BCE thousands of years of observation had taken place of the astronomical bodies, not least in Mesopotamia and Egypt, where in the former the so-called King's Watch observed the heavens every night for centuries, recording what they saw (Rochberg, 2016: chapter 7).

The Antikythera mechanism has revolutionized our appreciation of the mechanical and mathematical skills of the ancient Mediterranean world – prior to this, only a few rather crude gear wheels were known. There are some tantalizing references to Greek astronomical instruments, particularly Cicero, in his (now fragmentary) *De Re Republica,* written in 54 BCE, who describes a planetarium of Archimedes, as well as one other similar instrument (Yonge, 1877: 370–1):

> *I felt that the Sicilian geometrician must have possessed a genius superior to anything we usually conceive to belong to our nature. For Gallus assured us that the other solid and compact globe was a very ancient invention, and that the first model had been originally made by Thales of Miletus. . . . . He added that the figure of the globe, which displayed the motions of the sun and moon, and the five planets, or wandering stars, could not be represented by the primitive solid globe; and that in this the invention of Archimedes was admirable, because he had calculated how a single revolution should*

maintain unequal and diversified progressions in dissimilar motions. In fact, when Gallus moved this globe, we observed that the moon succeeded the sun by as many turns of the wheel in the machine as days in the heavens. From whence it resulted that the progress of the sun was marked as in the heavens, and that the moon touched the point where she is obscured by the earth's shadow at the instant the sun appears opposite.

The Antikythera mechanism condenses many long histories of human skills into one object. Skills in metal and wood working meet the mathematics of the time, together with the engineering necessary to create and put in place the gear wheels of the interior mechanism. Such histories fit into a Western notion of technical progress worked out through the history of instrument making, underpinned by the abstract manipulations of mathematics. The elements of the Antikythera story that do not so easily fit a history of technology are that we have no extant evidence of antecedents for such a device apart from the description given above, and geared mechanisms of similar sophistication are not seen again until the high Middle Ages. Our linear histories, in which the advances of one generation build upon those of their ancestors to be passed on to the future, do not easily work here. A further important caution is sounded by the presence of the zodiac on the front dial. The makers and users of this device lived in a universe which was much more sentient than our own. The five planets then known shaped and influenced the lives of humans from birth to death, mixing too with the more capricious influences of the gods. From the seventeenth century, in Europe science has often been in conflict with other belief systems, such as magic and religion (Thomas, 1971; Campion, 2009). The Greeks and Romans look like us in many ways, but in others they are profoundly different. Technologies exist within specific cultural situations and although elements get passed on there is severe filtering, so that only those elements which are helpful and enlightening are curated and developed.

What lessons does this story carry for us in a reconsideration of the history of technology? Some are straightforward – because the material record is so sparse, certain technologies can seem to appear with no known antecedents, and disappear without trace, even if this is not the case. As is shown above, other geared mechanisms are reported textually from the Classical Mediterranean, but so far only one major piece has been found – either they are still to be recovered, or they suffered the fate of much metal in the past – recycling. It also shows how a single find can completely change our perceptions of the knowledge and skills of the past. More fundamentally, it shows that we need to broaden the context of studies on the history of technology to include an attempt to understand how past people saw themselves and the world around them (material and otherwise). Although, using the modern (Western) worldview, we can 'explain' how things work – the mechanical ingenuity of the Antikythera mechanism, or processes such as the smelting of copper, in terms of chemistry, thermodynamics, and redox processes, this does not coincide at all with the frames of perception and explanation of the original participants. This observation immediately poses an interesting question to modern researchers in the field of ancient technologies: How can we understand the underlying perceptions of the practical procedures of ancient technological processes, when the original practitioners themselves would not recognize the modern definitions of the constituents and concepts which we use to describe them? We are essentially moving between two very different world views, without considering what might be inadvertently lost or created by such a transition. It is analogous to a language problem, where there is no agreed translation process. In particular, if we want to understand how and why technology changes, then we need to do it from their frames of reference – which is not to deny the importance of insights from our frame of reference, but simply to recognize that they are radically different.

Within what we might call this etic framework requiring us to enter the world of thought and practice of people in the past, understanding the process and motivation for technological innovation requires us to think about how people of the past acquired and incorporated new information into their worldviews, practices, skill sets, and culture. This concept of the acquisition of new knowledge and practice leads us to consider the role of 'accidental discoveries' and 'experimentation' compared to the receipt of material or knowledge from external sources. 'Accidental discovery' is a frequently used, but perhaps intellectually lazy, explanation for technological innovation. For an 'accidental discovery' to become an adopted technology, there has to be an observation on the part of the original practitioners that something different has happened, an appreciation that the new product fulfils a new need, or better fulfils an existing need, and, crucially, the process has to be reproducible. Perhaps only differing from this by degree, the role of 'experimentation' also deserves further examination. How do we differentiate 'accidental' production from deliberate 'experimentation' on the basis of the archaeological record alone? The answer to this probably involves large-scale studies of large assemblages of objects. More broadly, the relationship between intent, serendipity and outcomes needs some more serious thought, and brings in many interesting questions, largely focusing on 'what did the practitioners know and think about the world'? How did they tell this story to themselves? How did they think the world worked, particularly in the context of processes of transformation? How did they perceive and categorize animate and inanimate entities? In terms of technological innovation, when was there an intent to 'improve' a particular process? Or were there only ever unintended effects that were observed and opportunistically exploited? Until very recently, the common narrative of technological innovation has been largely predicated on the assumption that the primary motivation was an intentional and deliberate striving for specific technological improvement, but this may not always have been the case, especially if people did not work with a notion of technology congruent with our own. Recent scholarship has introduced the concept of 'anchored innovation', which pays much more attention to the social context of innovation, and in particular to 'horizontal' and 'vertical' anchoring, which implies considering relationships with contemporary or preceding practices (Sluiter, 2016). Other approaches are illustrated in the edited volume by Stockhammer and Maran (2017). Combining these ideas with that of an 'actor-centred' approach, we will also focus on the consequences of the observation that people themselves are shaped, physically and mentally, by the processes of making, so technology itself should be seen as a continuous dynamic dialog and interchange between humans and the material world. Questions of technology are therefore existential, rather than simply functional.

What Is Technology?

If the intention is to write something akin to a new 'history of technology', then we must first of all be clear about what we mean by 'technology'. Here we wish to take a much broader view of the definition of technology than has perhaps been the norm in the past, as exemplified in some of the major contributions reviewed below. At its simplest, and in common with most earlier studies, we take it to mean human knowledge and use of tools and crafts, and the processes by which material objects are made and used – in other words, the actions and materials which give rise to material culture. We see it as far more than this, however. We wish to go beyond the physical nature of objects and actions to understand the meaning and intentions of such objects and actions in their original contexts. This is simply to recognize that not all objects and actions (if, indeed, any) in human history have been imbued with the same rational, logical meanings that we ascribe to them from a twenty first century Western scientific perspective. Not to act on this recognition would effectively be to project our world picture backwards into very alien worlds, and which would inevitably lead to a misinterpretation of the underlying causes of technological change, and consequently would also repeat the worst failings of technological determinism. More positively, we argue that we cannot truly understand the motivations and choices made by earlier generations of scholars, inventors, technologists and artisans, if we do not attempt to see the world as they saw it or at least worked in it.

Simultaneously, we both accept and reject the modern concept of technology as a series of functional approaches to the world. An older notion would not divide technology from society, with the former concerning the practical and mechanistic elements of life, and the term society designating the world of social relations, mores and structures. Technology in this sense was often seen as the means by which people mobilised the energies of the world, with more efficient technology leading to a greater social complexity powered by higher levels of energy (Morris, 2010). There was plenty of scope for technological determinism here, with inventions and new deployments seen to be *causing* social change, rather than being an integral part of them. Systems theory in particular was prone to put 'society' in one box and 'technology' in another, and attempt to understand the relationship between the two (Binford and Binford, 1968; von Bertalanffy, 1968). However, there have always been a series of contradictory aspects to this notion. Within the word 'technology' is the root 'techne' applying to arts and crafts, designating the skills which created varied effects. People combine socially to create and enjoy such effects. Along with much current thought into materiality, we would make no separation between the technological and the social. All social relations involve making, using and exchanging material things. The technologies involved in making and using objects are linked to the skills of building and nuancing relations with people.

We acknowledge that the use of the term 'technology' has broadened considerably in recent years, breaking free from the old shackles of determinism, both cultural and technological. People now talk about the human body as technology, or explicitly consider variations in the techniques of the use of the body, drawing ultimately from the work of the French anthropologist, Marcel Mauss (2006), who was interested in deceptively simple questions such as why British and French soldiers were unable to use each other's shovels in the First World War (1914 CE–1918 CE). His answer was that people learned to use their bodies in ways that derived from cultural norms, but which are often unconsciously inculcated into them. While the basic mechanical properties of the human form, in terms of musculature and physiology, are fundamentally similar, they are deployed differently from one culture to another, and vary considerably over the course of individual lifetimes. Furthermore, the anthropologist Alfred Gell talked of art as a 'technology of enchantment', a set of forms which will vary from one culture to another, that derive from skilled practice and are designed to have a particular effect – to cause wonder or enchantment in the beholder. Gell's (1998) key question was not 'what does art mean?' but 'what does art do?' Art in this usage becomes part of the flows of power within society and a means of creating social relations with particular values. Finally, the notion of the 'cyborg' looks at the ways in which technologies are being introduced into the human body, in the form of pacemakers or even biochemical alterations through injections (Haraway, 1991). The blurring of the body and technology in the contemporary world makes us wonder whether technologies and bodies in the past were totally separate entities, or were indeed conjoined. Certainly the food we eat affects the biochemistry or musculature of the body, as does shelter, clothing and tool use. We might not want to go too far in blurring people and things, but there are questions to be asked concerning the conjoined nature of people and the material world. Such ideas are also found in so-called post-humanist thought, which critiques the unthinking emphasis on people as the centres of all the networks of relations they occupy (Agamben, 2004). Instead they insist that we should look at the totality of relations in a given situation and be open to the possibility that other species or forms of material have an influential effect. Human actions are then part of the networks of cause and effect rather than at their centre.

Following the above train of thought, we are fundamentally interested in the processes whereby humans can influence their material world, and, through the concept of materiality, the ways in which the material world can influence human behaviour. This brings into consideration, for example, processes such as the adoption of farming and the domestication of plants and animals, and the burial of the dead, for such new activities are either precipitated by new concepts in technology, or give rise to new concepts. We are very aware, however, that to extend the concept of technology to include such a definition begins to include the whole of archaeology and anthropology, and so we need to apply some limitations to prevent such a discussion becoming effectively endless. We will limit ourselves here to consider only the purely material culture aspects of such large-scale changes as the adoption of agriculture. The temptation to extend the concept of technology to cover all aspects of human existence, although attractive, has been somewhat reluctantly resisted, simply to give a boundary to the concept of a history of technology. Religious practice, for example, could be regarded as a technology – one which mediates the dialogue between this world and another, facilitated by a series of material artefacts, as well as a philosophical framework. For now, however, this temptation has been avoided.

The inception of pottery technology in particular has traditionally been seen as a key point in human technological development, originally associated with the development of agriculture and animal domestication. The earliest known fired clay artefacts consist of the assemblage of fired loess figurines (including the famous 11 cm tall so-called 'Venus figure') and other objects from the Palaeolithic site cluster at Dolni Věstonice and Pavlov in the Czech Republic (Vandiver et al., 1989), dated by radiocarbon to *c.*29,500–26,000 cal BCE. The earliest known pottery vessels were produced some 15,000 years later, apparently virtually simultaneously across a broad region of East Asia, including the Amur basin in Siberia, parts of southern China, and in Japan (Kuzmin, 2006, 2013). The largest number of sites containing early pottery are dated to the Incipient Jōmon period of Japan, the earliest of which is Odai Yamamoto I at *c*.15,250 cal BCE. Earlier still, however, are sites in South China, where one (Yuchanyan Cave) is reliably dated to 17,690–18,490 cal BP (15,740–16,540 cal BCE), making this currently the site of the oldest known pottery vessels in the world. Kuzmin (2013) lists 24 sites from North and South China, Japan, the Russian Far East and Trans-Baikal which have radiocarbon dates before 11,000 cal BP (*c*.9,000 BCE). Although in Western Asia and Europe we traditionally associate the origin of ceramics with the rise of agriculture and sedentism (the 'Neolithic Revolution'), these vessels considerably predate the Neolithic of East Asia, and their role in an essentially hunter-gatherer society remains something of a puzzle. Whatever the explanation, equating pottery with the first farming communities is anachronistic since in the regions listed above hunter-gatherer populations used pottery, whilst in other areas early farming communities were aceramic (e.g., the 'pre-pottery Neolithic' in the Near East). In other cultures, such as the Viking period on Orkney, pottery manufacture ceased because pottery became redundant as vessels were made from other materials. The causes of adoption and use (or disuse) of ceramics therefore varies according to regional social, economic and environmental factors. In the last ten thousand years (the Holocene) people further explored the plasticity of clay, in terms of the variety of form and decoration it allows and indeed encourages. Some of these possibilities are facilitated by the mineralogical structure of the clay itself, allowing manipulation and shaping when wet but considerable strength when fired, which demonstrates different creative potentials to those of wood, leather, or basketry (Gosden and Malafouris, 2015).

Technology and its history are often, however, considered solely through the study of its finest products and most skilled forms of production. The hand axe attracts attention, whereas the ordinary stone flakes do not; the Zhou ritual bronze vessel is more studied than every day metal tools of the same period; the Sutton Hoo helmet is analysed and discussed in greater detail than the cleats which held the Sutton Hoo boat together. Celebrating refined human skill and mastery of difficult and dangerous materials or processes does give us crucial insights into historical processes. However, these peak technical achievements of humanity can only emerge from the broad skills base of a society and cannot be understood in isolation.

Technology can be thought of as a commons. All human beings work with and through material culture, using things to shape the world, and in these processes the world they are shaping acts back to create them. In the contemporary world we variously use saucepans, plates, mugs, bicycles, chop sticks, lifts, canoes, and houses. Everyday skills are learnt in childhood and are taken for granted. It is only when we encounter something new – chopsticks for some, knives and forks for others – do we realize the difficulties involved in doing what others take for granted. Each society has its own range of material things (that we often label technology), and also an embodied set of skills in our hands, arms, legs, mouths, and the stances, orientations and movements of the whole body. Technology is equally made up of bodies and their skills as it is material things made of wood, fibre, clay, glass, or metal. We do not know the full range of things a body can do, nor have we exhausted the total range of possibilities in materials, either singly or in combination (Malafouris, 2013).

The technically extraordinary therefore emerges from the ordinary. A Zhou bronze was cast using very complex clay moulds into which the molten metal was poured. China has a 20,000 year history of ceramics and the control of fire through bonfires and increasingly sophisticated kilns. In the early history of Chinese pottery the skills of making and using pottery were widely shared, only becoming the province of specialists in the Neolithic when extraordinarily fine wares were created. The broadest controlled use of fire was for heating, lighting, and cookery, so that the taken-for-granted pyrotechnology used to cook an evening meal and keep people warm in the winter provided a broad familiarity with wood, dung, hearths and pots that was eventually refined and deployed by specialist potters and metalworkers. Such refinements could feed back too into the everyday, with metalworking perhaps influencing cookery. In any case, an understanding of what we now call chemistry, derived as much from how plants, animals and liquids react when cooked as any other area of life.

In summary, we wish to broaden the concept of technology away from a relatively narrow field of study which considers how tools were made and used, towards a more socially embedded study which considers the relationship between humans and the material world. This allows us to bring to bear developments in a range of related disciplines, including cognitive psychology and material culture theory, as well as to develop the concept of the 'actor-centred' focus on perception. In the light of this, we think that now is a good time to revisit the global history of technology. We believe that, by calling on an extended range of lenses, we can create a more holistic picture of the past, and derive new insights into the development and communication of technologies.

Earlier Approaches to the History of Technology

It is now nearly 70 years since the first volume in the monumental *History of Technology* series edited by Charles Singer (1876–1960), Eric J. Holmyard (1891–1959), and A. Rupert Hall (1920–2009) was published by the Clarendon Press, Oxford (Singer et al., 1954). The original vision (as explained in Singer, 1960) was for the period from 'Palaeolithic Times' to 1900 CE to be covered in five volumes, and these appeared between 1954 and 1958, with Trevor I. Williams (1921–1996) added as editor from volume 2 onwards (Singer et al., 1956, 1957, 1958a, 1958b). The series was extended to cover the technology of the first half of the twentieth century in two subsequent volumes edited by Williams alone (Williams, 1978).

The significance of this series, although much criticized at the time and subsequently, was profound. Singer himself, already recognized before embarking on this venture as a leading scholar in the history of medicine and science, was credited as having pioneered the history of technology as a new academic discipline, at least in the English-speaking world. His definition of the scope of his series, in the Introduction to volume 1 of *A History of Technology*, was 'how things are done or made'. The series was hailed as the 'definitive' publication on the history of technology, albeit one which focussed almost exclusively on the circum-Mediterranean world and adjacent regions. Although the histories of medicine and science (or at least of 'Natural Philosophy') had been deemed to be suitable subjects for academic discourse for several centuries, that of technology was only really addressed in the twentieth century. Earlier synthetic publications on technology, in the West from the eighteenth century onwards, had generally taken the form of Encyclopaedia, in which technological processes were described with a view to promoting technological 'progress'. Earlier practical manuals on specific technologies, such as mining, metal production, and glass-making, had been produced, notably in Germany, from the eleventh century onwards, becoming increasingly recognizable to modern eyes from the sixteenth century onwards. Obvious examples include Theophilus' *On Divers Arts* (*c.*1100 CE; Hawthorne and Smith, 1963), Agricola's *De Re Metallica* (1530 CE; Hoover and Hoover, 1912), Vannoccio Biringuccio's *De la Pirotechnia* (1540 CE; Smith and Gnudi, 1942) and Lazarus Ercker's *Beschreibung allerfürnemisten mineralischen Ertzt und Berckwercksarten* (1574 CE; Sisco and Smith, 1951). Nevertheless, they were clearly practical manuals, with no pretensions to recording technological change.

The influential nature of *A History of Technology* is reflected by the fact that an entire issue of the then newly established journal *Technology and Culture* (Vol. 1, part 4, 1960) was devoted to a critical evaluation of the first five volumes. A number of eminent scholars were asked to comment on specific areas of technology covered in the History. Many are instructively critical. In particular, Lewis Mumford warns against the temptation of 'forward-looking people' to be 'inclined to equate mechanical invention with civilization itself' (Mumford, 1960: 321). Significantly, he notes that 'as a history, it leaves everything to the reader' (Mumford, 1960: 322), by which he means that 'there is a vast difference between a series of monographs ... and a comprehensive technical history that would attempt to put these parts together in a fashion that would reveal interrelationships, possibly a pattern' (Mumford, 1960: 322–3). More specifically, other contributors point to errors and inconsistencies in the texts. For example, Lynn White, Jr notes some confusion in the treatment of the history of the crank-shaft ('The fact that this major history of technology can deal with the crank so cavalierly shows how inchoate the discipline still is' – White, 1960: 342), and also the history of the use of the horse ('While the treatment of the use of horses is extensive, it is often inaccurate' – White, 1960: 343).

Such criticisms from leading scholars might normally be expected to immediately condemn a published work to eternal oblivion, but that was not the case here. The overriding conclusion of even the most vocal critics was that, despite being a flawed product, it is one that nevertheless needs to exist. Mumford, somewhat grudgingly, notes that 'To those whose interest lies in a specialist field, this book has the virtues of a historical encyclopaedia' (Mumford, 1960: 322). Somewhat more generously, White, a specialist in medieval technology, notes that 'the second volume . . . is a milestone in the progress of our thinking about the Middle Ages' (White, 1960: 339). None of these criticisms would, however, have come as a surprise to the editors of the series. They were clearly aware of the shortcomings of the volumes. Singer subsequently published the original prospectus for the first five volumes, in which he identified three 'theoretical difficulties' (Singer, 1960: 306) in the creation of the series:

1. 'Technological skill is not closely related to "civilization" as that word is commonly understood'. To illustrate this, he refers to the technological sophistication of the material from the Sutton Hoo hoard, seen in the context of post-Roman Britain, thought of as a period of technological decline. This statement by Singer raises a whole raft of issues which require more detailed discussion, but it is not in principle an unreasonable observation. Sutton Hoo is an interesting example to have chosen, however, since it highlights the possible issues of temporal and spatial variation in technological skill. The objects found at Sutton Hoo could either have been preserved from an (more skilful) earlier period, or (more likely) imported from distant locations which had retained or developed specialist skills, thus rendering the immediate local link between 'technological skill' and 'civilization' less direct than the original comment appears to assume.

2. 'Technological periods, technological ideas, and the diffusion of technical devices cannot be separated as easily and distinctly as the periods, ideas, and diffusion of pure science'. This distinction between 'pure science' and 'technology' is presumably intended to highlight the difference between ideas and practice, but the point made here is potentially illusory, since the evidence for 'the periods, ideas, and diffusion of pure science' of necessity comes from written sources, with the associated appearance of having

spatial and chronological precision. In contrast, the evidence for techno-logical periods, ideas and diffusion comes primarily from material evidence, with the associated lack of spatial and chronological precision, making a direct comparison between the two complicated, to say the least.

3. 'The introduction and diffusion of technical devices – either with or without scientific foundation – must always have had some relation to general economic conditions'. From our perspective, this is an important but con-siderably understated recognition of the relationship between technology and 'economy'. Economy in this context is too restrictive a term, but our inclination would be to amplify this statement to positively emphasise the relationship between technological innovation and social conditions.

We might now feel that these 'theoretical difficulties', whilst representing a recognition of the complexity of the social contextualization of technology, do not go far enough, and do not pay sufficient attention to the broader cultural context. Nevertheless, we might agree with Singer's subsequent observation that 'Human affairs do not accommodate themselves exactly to centuries and "periods," though these abstractions are a necessity for purposes of exposition' (Singer, 1960: 307). Kranzberg, in his introduction to the special issue, states that 'Dr Singer himself was well aware of the shortcomings of those volumes; he regarded them not so much as a finished product, representing the "final word" in the history of technology, but rather as a beginning attempt which would stimulate and encourage further research and necessary scholarship' (Kranzberg, 1960: 302). We would certainly agree with, and applaud, this evaluation. With some hesitancy, it is our intention to pick up this challenge in this and subsequent volumes, thereby acknowledging the pioneering work of Singer and his colleagues.

The heavy European focus of *A History of Technology* was partially balanced by an equally monumental series, coincidently also first produced in 1954 (Needham and Wang L., 1954), in the form of *Science and Civilisation in China* edited by Joseph Needham (1900–1995). This series, published by Cambridge University Press, is considerably broader in scope than the 'History', and was structured differently to the work of Singer and his colleagues, in that it is a series of multipart volumes covering different topics. Volume 1 is an introduction; volume 2 describes the history of scientific thought in China; volume 3 covers 'Mathematics and the Sciences of the Heavens and Earth', with volume 4 being 'Physics and Physical Technology' (in three parts, including engineering). Volume 5 covers 'Chemistry and Chemical Technology' (currently in thirteen parts, ranging from paper technology to ceramic production). Volume 6 is 'Biology and Biological Technology' (in six parts), and volume 7 addresses

'Language and Logic'. Nearly seventy years later, this series now consists of twenty-seven substantial volumes, and is still growing. It has been condensed by Colin Ronan (1920–1995) in collaboration with Joseph Needham, into five volumes, entitled 'The Shorter Science and Civilisation in China' (Ronan, 1978–1995). These volumes cover China and Chinese science in volume 1, Mathematics, astronomy, meteorology and the earth sciences in volume 2, Magnetism, nautical technology, navigation, voyages (Vol. 3), Mechanical engineering, machines, clockwork, windmills, aeronautics (Vol. 4) and Civil engineering, roads, bridges, hydraulic engineering in volume 5.

It is hard to overestimate the significance of Needham's work, not only within China but also in a world context, in that it represents a sustained counterweight to the otherwise heavily Eurocentric narrative of the history of technology. It is deeply embedded in Chinese literature and philosophy, and his comparative approach, which greatly contributed to a widespread awareness of the contributions made by non-Western cultures and civilizations, deserves highlighting, since it can be seen as one of the major pioneering efforts in the development of a global approach. Some commentators (e.g., Major, 1975: 622) note that these works are 'as valuable in a topic on the history of Western science as for Chinese science itself', and also 'nothing like it exists for the history of Europe and, given the special conditions that produced Needham's masterwork, it is unlikely that there ever will be' (Finlay, 2000: 266). In his review of one of the volumes, Major (1975: 627) comments that the series is 'one of the boldest and greatest scholarly undertakings of our time'.

Nevertheless, Needham, like China itself, is a complicated subject to evaluate. Numerous reviews and tribute volumes have been published, including festchrifts by Teich and Young (1973), Li et al. (1982) and Said (1990), signifying recognition in Western, Chinese and Islamic cultural traditions. And yet reviews seem to be split. Many, if not most, subscribe to the views expressed above, and give *Science and Civilisation in China* the credit for bringing to world attention the many major contributions made in China which have influenced Western technology. Fairbank (1971: 329), in his review of Needham's work, identifies three 'packaged transmissions' from China to Europe – one about 1180 CE, consisting of the magnetic compass, the stern post rudder and the windmill, a second around the time of the Mongols involving the mechanical clock and gunpowder, and a third in the late 1300s CE involving the cast iron blast furnace, block printing, and iron chain suspension bridges. Other earlier contributions which could be named include paper, which reached the Islamic world in the eighth century CE, and Europe by the eleventh. Moreover, Needham is probably responsible for bringing the voyages of Zheng He (1405 CE–1433 CE) to Western attention (Finlay, 2000: 268–9). Other reviews (even from those who are generally supportive) have, however, been more critical, essentially blaming Needham's self-confessed love of China, together with his Marxist-Christian perspectives, for setting China and the West in opposition, and implicitly criticising Western civilisation (Finlay, 2000: 267). Needham, a biochemist by training, learnt his approach to the history of science from Charles Singer through their mutual interest in the history of medicine (Needham, 1981: x). Inevitably, given the time elapsed since the beginnings of *Science and Civilisation in China*, political and academic perceptions have changed. When Needham started his engagement with China in the late 1930s, China was still suffering from what it has called the 'century of humiliation' (*c*.1839–1949), and sinophiles such as Needham felt the need to redress the imbalances in perception. What Needham would make of modern China, set to resume its historical position as the leading economy in the world, is a matter for some speculation.

Academically, Needham has been criticised for a number of issues – for applying his Marxist belief that all cultural changes, including technology and science, are caused by changes in social structures (White and Spence, 1984: 173); never shying away from bold generalisations (Finlay, 2000: 268); not distinguishing between technology and science (Finlay, 2000: 266); 'engaging in a vast Sinophile work of special pleading' (Fairbank, 1971: 329), and under-playing the role of Buddhism in Chinese thought at the expense of Daoism (White and Spence, 1984: 177; Hsia and Schäfer, 2019: 98–9). Needham's own motivations and philosophy are explored by Finlay (2000), drawing on the remarkable biographical publication by Holorenshaw (1973), which turns out to be by Needham himself. He was, of course, a significant biochemist in his own right, before being introduced to Chinese scholarship by a group of visiting scientists at Cambridge in 1937. He threw himself into learning Chinese, and 'completely "fell in love" with Chinese civilization, finding it of inestimable value not only for its own sake but in the critical appraisal of his own' (Holorenshaw, 1973: 2). He saw himself as 'more free of cultural blind spots than most people' and dedicated his life to breaking down cultural barriers, stating that 'wisdom was not born with Europeans'. Twenty-five years after his death, and with *Science and Civilisation in China* still an ongoing project, many would see these as still necessary ideals, and recognize his contribution as a monumental achievement. The evaluation given by Lynn White, Jr probably captures most current views: 'I have emerged not in complete agreement with him, yet with a vastly increased sense of debt to him' (White and Spence, 1984: 171).

Perhaps the greatest legacy of *Science and Civilisation in China* is the articulation of what has become known as 'the Needham question' – why did China cease to develop technologically from the early Ming dynasty (*c*. fourteenth century CE), after being at the forefront for much of the preceding periods?

(Perdue, 2006; O'Brien, 2009). More specifically, Needham asked 'Why did the scientific revolution not begin in China' (Needham, 1960: 301–8). This question 'haunted' Needham (Perdue, 2006: 176), and runs like a thread through much of his scholarship. It has spawned a huge literature, in which some attribute it to the lack of interest in innovation on behalf of Confucianist scholars – an idea dismissed by White and Spence (1984: 177) – whereas others have deflected the question by saying that China shifted attention away from technology to the establishment of the world monetary system by adopting a silver-based economy based on Spanish silver from the Americas during the Ming (Sun et al., 2021). The debate continues.

Another major series of work, essentially in the Anglophone tradition, comes from Robert J. Forbes (1900–1972), who started his career as a chemist with Royal Dutch Shell, became interested in the history of the use of bitumen and asphalt, and was subsequently appointed Professor in the History of Applied Science and Technology at the University of Amsterdam in 1947. Between 1940 and 1950 he published in Dutch a bibliographic series in 10 parts entitled *Bibliographia Antiqua: Philosophia Naturalis*, with a further 2 supplementary volumes in 1952 and 1963. The subjects covered were eclectic: Part 1, Mining and geology (1940); part 2, Metallurgy (1942); parts 3 and 4, Building materials; Pottery, faience, glass, glaze, beads (1944); parts 5 to 8, Paints, pigments, varnishes, inks and their application; Leather, manufacture and application; Fibrous materials; Paper, papyrus, and other writing materials (1949); part 9, Man and nature (1949); part 10, Science and technology (1950). Between 1955 and 1964 he published a second series of books in English, entitled Studies in Ancient Technology, in nine volumes, which can therefore also be added to the Anglophone cannon. These form a wide ranging series, with the following contents:

- Volume 1 – Bitumen and petroleum in antiquity; The origin of alchemy; Water supply (1955a).
- Volume 2 – Irrigation and drainage; Power; Land transport and road-building; The coming of the camel (1955b).
- Volume 3– Cosmetics and perfumes in antiquity; Food, alcoholic beverages, vinegar; Food in classical antiquity; Fermented beverages 500 B.C.–1500 A. D.; Crushing; Salts, preservation processes, mummification; Paints, pigments, inks and varnishes (1955c).
- Volume 4– The fibres and fabrics of antiquity; Washing, bleaching, fulling and felting; Dyes and dyeing; Spinning; Sewing, basketry and weaving; Weaving and looms; Fabrics and weavers (1956).
- Volume 5 – Leather in antiquity; Sugar and its substitutes in antiquity; Glass (1957).

- Volume 6 – Heat and heating; Refrigeration, the art of cooling and producing cold; Light (1958).
- Volume 7 – Ancient geology; Ancient mining and quarrying; Ancient mining techniques (1963).
- Volume 8 – Metallurgy in antiquity, part 1: Early metallurgy, the smith and his tools, gold, silver and lead, zinc and brass (1964a).
- Volume 9 – Metallurgy in antiquity, part 2: Copper and bronze, tin, arsenic, antimony and iron (1964b).

It is important to recognize that the Western Anglophone tradition of the history of technology, represented most obviously in the works of Singer et al., is not the only approach to the subject. Given the major contribution made by the French school of anthropology to the theory of material culture, and the long tradition of technical encyclopaedia in France from the eighteenth century onwards, it is perhaps surprising to note the lack of a systematic synthesis of the history of technology from a French perspective until the 1960s. Daumas, the editor of a five volume work produced between 1962 and 1998, entitled *Histoire générale des techniques*, noted that 'in the French language, there is no satisfactory general work on the history of technology, although much has been written about it – indeed, too much has been written about a subject about which, on the whole, there is little known' (Daumas, 1960: 415). The first two volumes of this work (*Les Origines de la Civilisation Technique* (Daumas, 1962) and *Les Premieres Etapes Du Machinisme* (Daumas, 1965)) deal with the pre-modern world, and were translated into English by Eileen Hennessy as *A History of Technology & Invention: Progress through the Ages, Vol. 1 The Origins of Technological Civilization* (1969a) and *Vol. 2 The First Stages of Mechanization* (1969b). Daumas uses the term 'techniques' rather than technology, which he defines as 'those human activities whose object it is to collect, adapt, and transform raw materials in order to improve the condition of human existence' (Hennessy, 1969a: Vol. 1, p. 7). The overall approach is unapologetically progress-driven – indeed, Daumas uses the need for progress to distinguish humans from other species. He contends that humans are characterized by the 'constant need for progress, which has never slackened since the beginning of the Quaternary era' (Hennessy, 1969a: Vol. 1, p. 1). Although we would dispute this, at least for large regions of the world, we find more commonality with other aspects of Daumas' approach. In particular, we welcome the emphasis placed by Daumas and co-authors on the role of personal contact in transmitting technological innovation, and the link to demography – the observation that population density is an important parameter in technology transmission and innovation. This, according to Daumas, explains why the rise of cities from the Neolithic onwards accelerates that rate of change of technology (Hennessy, 1969a: Vol. 1, p. 4). Interestingly,

Daumas also highlights what has subsequently become known as the 'Needham question', discussed above.

It is perhaps even more surprising to see that, with one exception, there is little in the way of a systematic synthesis of the history technology in the German literature, given the pre-eminence of Germany in mining and metal-working technology, and the fact that most of the European practical techno-logical literature from the eleventh century onwards comes from German scholars – for example, Theophilus (Hawthorne and Smith, 1963), Agricola (Hoover and Hoover, 1912), Ercker (Sisco and Smith, 1951). The exception noted above is the work of Feldhaus (1914, 1928, 1931), although the last of these, *Die Technik der Antike und des Mittelalters*, was described as 'erratic and undocumented' by White (1960: 339).

Also written in German, Svorykin (transliterated as Zvorykin, Zvorikine, or Sworikyn) and co-workers published a Russian (Soviet era) view on the history of technology (Svorykin et al., 1962). As explained by Svorykin (Zvorikine, 1960, 1961), the differences between a Western and a Soviet approach to the history of technology are summarized as:

1. differences in understanding the essence of technology and its 'laws of development'
2. differences in the period division of the history of technology, and
3. differences in presentation for individual periods.

In elaborating the differences in understanding, Svorykin firstly quotes from Gordon Childe's contribution to Singer et al.'s *A History of Technology* (Vol. 1, chapter 2), in which Childe (1954) states 'Technology should mean the study of those activities directed to the satisfaction of human needs which produce alterations in the material world. In the present work the meaning of the term is extended to include the results of those activities'. Zvorikine (1960: 422) asserts that 'Soviet authors take a somewhat different view of the essence of technology and its laws of development. ... . Soviet scholars center their attention not on human activities, but on the implements of labor. ... '. In his summing up, the history of technology is described as 'a branch of learning dealing with the development of implements of labor within the system of social production'. The emphasis on 'laws of development' provides an interesting historical perspective, and raises generic issues about the degree to which a socially embedded activity can be thought of as subject to any universal laws. Similarly, the focus on 'implements of labor' seems too narrow to the contemporary perspective, since it restricts the history of technology to a largely mechanical activity, ignoring many of the issues raised above, deriving as it does from a particular reading of Marx.

Following from the above brief descriptions, it is clear that the time has come to revisit this topic, not least because of the many new archaeological discoveries made since the 1960s. However, as noted in the previous sections, there are other equally compelling reasons for a reappraisal. Many of the pioneering works described above were, of necessity, content to simply document progress and map out directions of travel. This is exactly as it should be, since without such a map it is impossible to move towards a more synthetic viewpoint. The underlying philosophy of many of these works which investigated the materials science aspect of technology, however, was that there was something inherently inevitable about technological development – something akin to an expression of the British Victorian virtue of 'progress' – and something which is therefore susceptible to a modern rational explanation. This is a clear manifestation of technological determinism – a model which assumes that the direction of travel is dictated by the physical properties of the materials themselves, without social or cultural influence. As explained above, we do not wish to follow this road, and will not therefore be producing a history of technology in the older sense of these words. Drawing on developments in anthropology and the area now known as 'science and technology studies' (STS: e.g., Hackett, 2008; Sismondo, 2010), it has become clear that the traditional material-property based explanations for the development and adoption of new technologies are in general completely inadequate to understand this aspect of human development. By breaking away from these older notions of functionalism and of 'technological progress', we hope to uncover the idiosyncratic variety of human relationships with the world. Ultimately, given the depth of human entanglements in the material world, which are unusual compared to any other species, we are asking what makes us human, and what is our relationship to the non-human?

Varying Theoretical Approaches to the History of Technology

There have been various reactions to technology over the last few centuries, from the Enlightenment-derived worries over the influence of the machine to those that celebrate technological advance as a driving force for progress in the contemporary world. These can be rather crudely divided into romantic reactions or humanities and social science-based approaches, and latterly to more scientific or technological approaches. We wish to describe briefly the genealogy of all of these, before attempting to explore and extend these various approaches in subsequent volumes.

In Table 1 we have laid out a broad division of varying approaches and thinkers to the issue of technology. This is aimed to be illustrative of different

Table 1 A rough typology of approaches to technology. The columns indicate broad sensibilities in people's writing and thought from the eighteenth century to the present, with the oldest groups/individuals at the top of the table

Romantic	Enlightenment	Social Science/ Science	Scientific
	French Encyclopaedists		
Ruskin	Marx		Thomsen/Worsaae
Arts and Crafts			
			Pitt Rivers
Heidegger	Mauss	Cyril Stanley Smith	White, Steward and the evolutionists
	Bourdieu	Henry Hodges?	Most of Processual Archaeology
Ingold	Sennett	Science and Technology Studies	Complexity theorists

tendencies in thought and approach, rather than any definitive summing up of these. Indeed, many of those in the column labelled 'Romantic' might well deny that they are interested in technology at all, preferring notions such as making, but then looking at the processes of life as being part-and-parcel of making (see Ingold, 2011, 2013).

The Romantics (old and new) have worried about the effects of mass-living, mass-production and mass-consumption on human communities and sensibilities. Ruskin's desire to return to smaller organic communities of the type found in the medieval period was quixotic, but continues a strand of thought in which the labour needed to produce things we might designate as 'art', as well as more everyday forms, should be honoured and valued for the skills it represents. Honouring skilled human labour in all its forms is an impetus to much archaeology and anthropology of technology and techniques in ways that link the human body and its products (e.g., Fox, 1958). Already, here the neat lines of our typology become blurred, as there are overlaps with the interests of Mauss (1979, 2006) in the habitus of the body resulting in skilled performances and more tangible products. Also in our romantic column is Heidegger's reaction against modern, technocratic engagements with the world, which he saw as leading to inauthentic modes of being (Heidegger, 1977). Heidegger saw technology as revealing vital elements of human placement within the world, helping to foster the broad phenomenological approach within archaeology and anthropology, which is less often about making and using objects and more often about movement, perception, and engagement, that is the nature and content of human experience.

We have distinguished romantic and enlightenment approaches in our table, as the latter look at the forms of logic that emerge in human action, which might either be coded in a formal logical manner or be seen as a more diffuse cultural logic. In the latter case, Mauss's notion of *habitus*, taken up and developed by Bourdieu (1990), is central to later discussion. Here the logics of the body and of culture more generally mingle around the problem of how people make sense of their worlds. Cultural logics ultimately derive from human action in the world, often very mundane forms, such as the use of various shovels for digging, or indeed the ways in which people walk, which vary culturally. *Habitus* for both Mauss and Bourdieu is learned in our earliest years, so that in Bourdieu's words, it is not something we know, but something we are.

Marx has been crucial to many sets of debates around technology, for instance in the Soviet approaches mentioned above and predominantly through the work of Childe in Western traditions – for instance Childe (1936). Marx's scheme of modes of production was a device to provide a series of historical stages for social change based around changes in production (Marx, 1867). A mode of production was divided into the forces of production (itself divided into human labour and the means of production, i.e., the technical means at the disposal of society) and the relationships of production – the patterns of ownership of both the means of production and the outputs. This latter aspect brought in issues of class, power, and social benefit which were central to Marx's analysis. His evolutionary scheme of primitive, ancient, feudal, capitalist, and socialist modes of production, leading eventually to communism, is now followed by very few, but the broader theoretical underpinnings still have considerable relevance and currency, but was echoed by other thinkers such as Lewis Henry Morgan (1877). Marx's general conception that production is also consumption, using up raw materials in the process of making new things which then in their turn will be consumed, highlights the cyclical nature of production and consumption. Marx also highlighted the reciprocal effects of people and labour: in producing material forms people developed and deployed their own skills and, in consequence, produce themselves as cultural beings. Production and technology have an existential element for Marx, together with politics and economics, ensuring that technology cannot be thought of in purely technical terms, nor as having a deterministic effect on society. The concept of reproduction reinforced the cyclical and multidimensional nature of production and consumption. From one generation to the next, cultural forms needed to reproduce themselves and reproduction includes human beings as people who work and consume, as well as the renewing or curating the technical means of production and the gaining of supplies of raw materials. In ensuring these elements of reproduction, cultural forms also reproduce the political and economic dimensions of life, which determine who does the work, who owns the technology and the products, and hence the nature of benefit or exploitation in varying cultural forms. Reproduction never brings about exact replication, so that each generation of people and materials differs from the previous, analogous to descent with modification (the influence of Darwin on Marx is perceptible). The process-driven nature of Marx's view is still important today.

Materials intervene with and direct human action to some extent, so that new things arise out of an interaction between people and materials, rather than arising from the inherent inventiveness of people. Furthermore, following Mauss, materials 'enskill' people. The development of a new game, such as tennis or cricket, requires a complex range of muscular actions deriving from the racket/bat and the court/pitch which have never arisen before, as well as new cognitive connections between eye, brain, and muscle. An Ice Age hunter had sets of skills appropriate to their prey, terrain, and technology, which may well not exist today in exactly the same form. Materials are plastic, but so too is the human body and the skills of action and perception vary greatly through space and time (Manitsaris et al., 2014). One study of traditional pottery-making skills compared the manual dexterity of French and Indian potters, showing that on average the Indian potters used 30 per cent more forms of hand movement (Gandon, 2011). The work of Richard Sennett (2009) extends the notion of craft to many areas of modern life, extolling the importance of care, skill and thoughtful engagement as key elements of life currently under threat in all areas of life, from conventional craft production to cooking to childcare or office work. Sennett is also centrally interested in how people act and experience as a group, coming together in joint projects and using shared skills.

A key question to be answered is whether these technologies predate, and thereby enable, social change, or whether they in fact follow it, and are therefore a consequence of it – an issue focussed on in several papers within the edited volume by Stockhammer and Maran (2017). The traditional view is that an increased effectiveness in key activities such as warfare and food production is created by the technological progression from stone to iron, and that therefore these may be highly significant factors in one particular group's ability to feed itself, or to defend itself and wage war upon its neighbours. Such views are predicated upon the idea that human needs and desires are constant, with technology more or less able to meet those needs. Obviously, there are baseline requirements of the human organism, in terms of water, nutrition, shelter and social relations which need to be met to ensure survival. Most societies are able to live way beyond such baseline requirements most of the time (in fact it may only be in the last few centuries that things like famine are a constant threat to people), so that such basic requirements are not determining forces. Instead, there is a good deal of plasticity in the relations between people and things, with new things giving rise to new desires, skills, and capabilities (Malafouris, 2013). There are two important issues here. First, the development of something new extends and changes people, so that mobile phones and computers, separately and in combination, are providing new dimensions for people to expand into, allowing forms of communication and information flow which were unthinkable a few decades ago. The second point is linked to this – the physical constitution of materials offers a space of possibility within which people can explore and develop – the firing of clay is channelled and constrained by the nature of clay minerals, its additions, water content, and so on.

A more science-based approach to the question of technological innovation is found in the work of Cyril Stanley Smith (1903–1992). Smith had a most varied career, working on the Manhattan Project amongst other things and ending his working life as emeritus professor of metallurgy and humanities at MIT, which demonstrates some of the range of his interests. Primarily a metallurgist, he became interested in the history of metallurgy after his marriage to Alice Marchant Kimball, a social historian, in 1931. Subsequently, in collaboration with John G. Hawthorne, Anneliese G. Sisco, Martha Teach Gnudi, and others, he produced some of the definitive translations of and commentaries on many of the Classical and medieval technological treatises. His interest in archaeological materials derived from a desire to understand the links between the nature and structure of matter (especially that of metals) and the nature and abilities of the human body (e.g., Smith, 1981). For Smith, artefacts were central, with the developing techniques of modern science able to analyse form and microstructure in a manner which led to new elements of cultural understanding. Technology, for Smith, was dynamic and involved not just the skills of making but also those of appreciation, bringing in questions of the sensory and emotional reactions to artefacts.

Another way of thinking about the interactions between people and things is through the notion of the assemblage, exemplified in the work of Bruno Latour (1993, 2005) and others, in which people and things are not separated but interconnected within networks of mutual influence. Given the complex interactions between people and things, Latour (2005) emphasises that it is important to avoid a priori judgements about what things or people are capable of in any given situation, and argues that these capabilities must be established empirically. Such views have helped give rise to 'Science and Technology Studies' (STS: e.g., Hackett, 2008; Sismondo, 2010) which attempt to get away from that idea that science is either wholly objective – that correct observation and experiment by an appropriately trained researcher will lead to the correct conclusions – or entirely socially constructed – that the politics or culturally constructed worldviews of the observers determine the conclusions reached. All views, scientific or otherwise, are culturally constructed to some degree, but there are aspects of ways in which the world works that can surprise us and influence our conclusions; it is the subtle interplay between human relations and material relations and observations that influences how both science works and technologies are deployed.

Technological change has been basic to defining chronological periods in archaeology, most prominently the Three Age system (Rowley-Conwy, 2007). We have become accustomed to seeing technological change as the defining metric for human development – from the 'Stone Age' through to the 'Bronze' and 'Iron' Ages. Beyond creating a basic relative chronology, however, it is now widely accepted that such terminology is grossly misleading. The defining characteristic of Bronze Age society was almost certainly not the ability to smelt copper alloys – it is much more likely to have been related to population size and social organization, and the relationships between different groups of people. This is accepted, of course, in our use of the terms Mesolithic and Neolithic – where their definitions depend partly on the types of stone tools made and used, but the major shift between the two is thought to be the adoption of a settled agricultural lifestyle. This then prompts the question 'what role did the characteristic titular technologies of bronze and iron have in society?' A conventional view is that, because bronze is assumed to be technologically superior to stone, and iron to bronze, then an Iron Age society is somehow 'superior' to that of the preceding Bronze Age – a view given credence by the almost universal observation that the use of iron succeeds that of bronze, and replaces it in some key functions such as tool and weapon manufacture (except in Africa, of course). Whilst it is certainly true that in some limited (but nonetheless significant) spheres iron and steel technically outperform bronze (as bronze does stone), it is clearly overly simplistic to assume that this succession of technology is the dominant force in societal evolution. From Worsaae to Pitt Rivers to White and Steward there were attempts to order human history through a series of technological stages, where technological change also powered the movement between social forms, from band to tribe to chiefdom to state.

Such technologically driven notions of history were also central to processual archaeology from the 1960s onwards, in the work of Binford (Binford and Binford, 1968), Flannery (1972) and, in a more complicated manner, David

Clarke (1968). Processual archaeology still forms an important strand of the discipline today.

Cultural Logics and Materials

All societies have a variety of ways of understanding cause and effect. In the Western world we can see that magic, religion, and science have all been used at various times to explain the natural world and human engagements with and within it. Each of these approaches still have adherents and practitioners today. Magic refers to human interventions in physical processes (Gosden, 2020); religion explores divine interventions in the world, and science is a mode of enquiry exploring the physical or biological aspects of the world, often within a rather mechanistic model of cause and effect. We now tend to treat each of these approaches as mutually exclusive, and project this separation onto the past. For instance, in discussions around Stonehenge there are a number of separate conversations, some of which concern the ritual or religious role of the monument on the one hand, or the issues of how the stones were moved and erected on the other. Those making and using Stonehenge would not have separated these lines of thought and action but would have thought more holistically about how to construct and use the various phases of the monument. A key element of understanding technology is to grasp difference in the cultural logics varying groups apply to materials. E. B. Tylor's synthetic work, *Primitive Culture* (1871), put forward an evolutionary scheme for the history of human thought and understanding which saw a linear progression from magic to religion to science. The first of these terms designated a mode of operation and understanding in which people attempted to intercede with and manipulate the spiritual powers of the world through secret spells and arcane acts. His notion of magic was linked to the idea of animism, in which it was thought that the world contains a large number of powers and spirits inhabiting various plants, animals, and objects that might then be animate and able to intervene in human lives. Magic and animistic beliefs differed from religions, in which powers were concentrated in one or more divine beings who needed to be supplicated through prayer. Both of these were essentially false understandings of the way in which the world works, according to Tylor, with a truer understanding only coming about with the rise of modern science. Lévy-Bruhl (1926) took a similar line, summing up so-called 'primitive' thought as one of participation, which posits the consubstantiality of people and things, whereby the same set of processes are seen to animate the world as a whole, whether the human or the non-human element. We can say that there are various basic human orientations to reality, one of which emphasises causality and the other participation. Both modes of understanding are found in all human cultural forms, but in a different balance.

Lévy-Bruhl's views find echoes in the work of a number of influential later writers who, covering similar intellectual ground, also emphasise the entangled nature of people and of things. More recent examples include Ingold (2000), Stengers (2000), Latour (2005), and Hodder (2013). The difference between these twenty first century views and those of researchers at the beginning of the preceding century is that the nature of human-material engagements has become a more active focus of research rather than mere passive markers of change in the inexorable development of human thought.

Latour (2005) has developed what he calls 'symmetrical anthropology' in which he says that, in any analysis, things and people must both be included and that we should not prejudge the capacities of either, especially as we in the west tend to think of people as active and objects as passive. More animistic notions of things should be encouraged, he argues, so that we can look at under what circumstances things will have a determinant effect on people. Drawing inspiration from animistic forms of thought in looking at the relations between people and things, Tim Ingold (2000) wants to shift our basic set of images about the world and people, together with the language used to describe it. He uses metaphors of growth and development to look at the manner in which people grow into sets of relationships with plants, animals, and materials in ways which effectively change all the actors (human and non-human) and objects involved. Human capabilities come about in the context of particular sets of relationships between humans, things, and the natural world, embodied through play, performance, and labour in a manner which dissolves fixed divisions between culture and nature. Intelligence is imagination enacted, coming into being through work in the world, so that thought and reflection are dependent upon people's action rather than actions being directed by mental structures.

Descola (2013) lays out three different ways of conceiving of the world – animism, totemism, and naturalism. The last of these is perceived as the Western view, dividing nature (to be investigated by the physical or biological sciences) from culture (probed by social sciences and humanities). This perception is historically situated, emerging only in the last few hundred years. Totemism takes the differences between natural species as a model for social distinctions – an Aboriginal clan might take the kangaroo as their totem, attributing to themselves some of the characteristics of that animal, as distinct from other groups with other animals as their totems. Animism sees continuity between humans and natural things, with the attribution of human characteristics and dispositions to animals and objects. Rocks and trees, jaguars or elk, being animate and intentioned, can have many of the attributes of human reason, albeit in ways which are specific to the kinds of things they are.

Although there are significant differences in the specific approaches taken by Ingold, Latour, Descola, and others, they are more or less united in their attempts to understand human life as developing in partnership with the world. Furthermore, each has a commitment to understanding complexity, feeling that no single viewpoint, theory, or approach can adequately account for the world in all its multiplicity. We hope that the new views of technology which will emerge in this series will display varied viewpoints and approaches to making and using material things.

Part of this partnership with the world has involved alchemy – commonly seen in both East and West as the search for the 'Philosopher's Stone' with which to transform base metals into gold, but also, particularly in Daoist China, seen as the search for the elixir of immortality. It was, however, much more than this, and essentially encapsulated all approaches to experimental chemical sciences, but based on a different perception of the nature of materials. For too long has alchemy popularly been seen as incoherent, irrational, obscure, and deluded, but this is clearly not always the case. It was completely coherent and rational, although sometimes intentionally made obscure, providing that the world was seen through Aristotelean eyes, in which matter was composed of four qualities (air, earth, fire, and water), and transmutation could be effected by adding or removing some of these qualities (Pollard, 1988; Linden, 2003; Principe, 2007; Martinón-Torres, 2011). A similar set of considerations apply to the development of alchemy in China, based on an equivalent perspective of the five-fold nature of matter (Needham, 1971; Chikashige, 1976).

A definition of the term 'manufacture' given by Sir Juland Danvers in 1893 in his evaluation of the state of manufacture in India rather fortuitously leads us to a consideration of the link between technology and alchemy: 'The term manufacture may be taken as meaning the transformation of an original substance, by the dexterity of manual labour, into articles for the use of man'. (Danvers, 1893: 602). This emphasis on transformation takes us immediately into the world of alchemy, the role of which is central to understanding the history of technology. No lesser scholar than Cyril Stanley Smith embraced this view:

> *Transmutation was a thoroughly valid aim, a natural outgrowth of Aristotle's combinable qualities, and its truth was demonstrated by every child growing from the food he ate, by every smelter who turned green earth into red copper or black galena into base lead or virgin-hued silver, by every founder who turned copper into gleaming yellow brass, by every potter who glazed his ware, by every goldsmith who produced niello, by every maker of stained glass windows, and by every smith who controlled the metamorphosis of iron*

during its smelting, conversion to steel, and hardening. Such changes of
properties, seen physically, are transmutations, but they are not chemical in
the purified modern sense . . . . (Smith, 1968: 639)

Such a view, especially when combined with the idea that the technological transformations listed by Smith would have appeared 'magical' to the uninitiated observer, reinforces the idea that we should not ignore the role of alchemy (and magic) in the history of technology.

Spatial and Temporal Orders of Technology

Technologies have their own sets of spatial and geographical orders, which are connected to the regions over which they are shared, the boundaries between one technological zone and another, and the manner in which innovations are embraced or resisted. We can start to understand the broad and changeable geographies of material culture and techniques by mapping their distribution over time. To generalize considerably, we can see the Palaeolithic as being a period in which technologies were very widely shared. This is most obvious through early forms of stone tools, such as hand axes, but is also apparent in the Upper Palaeolithic in the distributions of very specific stone-working techniques (e.g., microblade industries in East Asia). In places like Europe there were a succession of cultural forms with similar sets of bone, stone, and clay technologies (which presumably had echoes in organic forms that survive rarely). In the Neolithic, from the Middle East to central and eastern Asia and west to Europe, a mosaic of cultural forms developed that produced a great range of forms of pottery, stone, domestic architecture, and relationships with plants and animals, even though the broad set of raw materials from which variety was generated were the same. This produces a world of cultural variability with which we are much more familiar in the present day. To make this point is not to say that Palaeolithic forms of life were lacking in any way, but merely that difference and material engagements were constituted in an interestingly different manner, perhaps linked in some way to the relatively low levels of population with their greater degrees of mobility. The more diverse 'Neolithic mosaic' emerges from a range of experiments with material forms and, although there was obviously trade between groups, difference was exaggerated and possibly prized. Social differences were reinforced by the absence of some of the modes of transport that we take for granted in later periods – the horse, the camel, carts, and chariots, and ocean going boats were either absent or of relatively limited use.

The end of the Neolithic sees the spread of geographically broader sets of material culture, such as the distribution of Corded Ware and Beaker pottery in

Europe, which may be associated with the wider adoption of new forms of transport. The succeeding Bronze Age sees both difference and the effect of distance decline, with greater personal mobility likely. Widespread cultural forms are found in many areas, differentiated and characterised by differences in pots and metalwork. In some limited areas there are centralisations of population that we now call towns. The towns of Mesopotamia were the sites of a great burst of technical innovation with the development of the fast potting wheel, granulation and filigree in metalwork, and many more monumental forms of building, to be echoed also in Egypt with the development of glass, and technologies of iconography and local forms of building, most famously the pyramids. It seems likely, as discussed below, that the increased levels of social contact afforded by living in sedentary towns gave rise to greater opportunities for technological innovation and adoption. Rather later, in the towns of Shang China, long familiarity with the high temperatures utilised in pottery making, including early porcelain, became the basis for some of the most complex forms of bronze working (Figure 2). In all cases, these changes were linked to new ritual systems and the emergence of elite cultures.

The Bronze Age also saw materials that could be regularly recycled, primarily bronze itself, but also gold, silver and glass. Finished forms could be reworked into new forms and material could move through space and over time. Effective distances diminished with new technologies of transport and it is possible that the movement of bulk goods occurred for the first time, especially by boat.

The succeeding Iron Age saw the emergence of new large power blocks in some areas, providing a new impetus for the creation of materials for display, personal adornment and ritual. In other areas, such as the steppe zone, some groups became more mobile as a consequence of the adoption of the horse, helping to facilitate the movement of ideas, techniques and materials. The interactions between sedentary and mobile populations take on important dynamics that last down to the present, although concepts of purely sedentary or completely mobile groups of people may well be over-simplistic.

Just as there are important questions about how technologies, materials, and artefacts are distributed over space, the same is true of transmission through time. The *longue durée* provides a long backdrop of change, over which new technologies are introduced and experimented with. A new technology, such as weaving or glass making provides novel dimensions of possibility within which people can experiment and explore. Exploration of the possibilities inherent in a particular new material or technique is probably much more significant than its invention (Bender Jørgensen et al., 2018), despite the greater emphasis that is often placed on origins by archaeologists. In any cultural context the process of reproducing the technological basis of society is necessary and ongoing.

Figure 2 Tripod cauldron (Ding), 1200 BC–1100 BC. (Heritage Images/Hulton Archive/Getty Images)

Reproduction involves replicating the technical basis of production, acquiring the necessary raw materials and ensuring the human skills base is maintained from one generation to the next. Reproduction is constant and rarely occurs without change. Where this is possible, the process of reproduction recycles older forms of materials into new variations, which are incorporated within existing themes (Bray et al., 2015; Pollard et al., 2018). Each technology has its own set of sequences and temporalities, most effectively brought out in the studies of the *chaîne opératoire,* discussed below. Although this approach has frequently been applied to the study of archaeological pottery (Tite, 1999) and stone tools (Shott, 2003), it has also been used, particularly in the Mediterranean area, on a wide range of other materials (Brysbaert, 2011), including metal production (e.g., Georgakopoulou et al., 2011).

Another dimension to consider in relation to transmission over time is the tendency of many luxury objects to become a necessity, as pointed out by Childe (1954: 38). He noted that 'Human needs are not fixed and immutable, nor yet innate'. This is clear in the modern day – those of us who remember the introduction of the 'speaking brick' (otherwise known as a so-called mobile phone!) will recall the cost and weight of these devices in the 1980s and 1990s, and yet they are now indispensable, if not always cheap. Many if not most objects and practices in the past must have gone through a similar assimilative process.

How Does Technology Change?

A great deal of thought and ink has been expended on trying to explain and understand the processes of technological innovation and diffusion. Not only is such an understanding important from a historical perspective, but it is also of crucial importance in the modern world, where for many countries the entire industrial strategy is now linked to developing innovation and entrepreneurship. The dimensions to this discussion are vast, ranging from the significance of individual inspiration giving rise to 'invention', to the responsive mode of problem-solving as the driver for innovation. Beyond this are considerations of the context of innovation, which vary from complete isolation from any related activity, to a complex process of co-creation. As a third dimension, the concept of continuous innovation as opposed to spontaneous creation provides a temporal axis to the discussion. Such considerations are particularly important in an archaeological context, where ideas of technological innovation and diffusion are fundamental to interpreting the archaeological record. Significant questions include where and when was a particular process first 'invented', and the related question of whether significant innovations were invented once and subsequently diffused elsewhere, or whether multiple parallel innovations have taken place. Whilst recognizing the fundamental challenge of ever identifying the first occurrence of anything tangible in the archaeological record, let alone the presence of something as intangible as an idea, it is true to say that some of the most critical events in human history, including animal domestication and agriculture (Darwin, 1868; Barker, 2006; Zeder, 2008), and the smelting of metals (Tylecote, 1976; Roberts et al., 2009; Roberts and Thornton, 2014), have been the subject of such debates. Apart from noting that some human societies, covering large times and regions, have not engaged with such innovations (and have consequently and unhelpfully in the past been branded as 'uncivilized' by those who have), the general opinion in many of these debates is that multiple independent innovation seems common. Unless one returns to older ideas of prehistoric 'hyper-diffusionism' (such as those encapsulated by Elliot Smith (1915), in which most 'inventions' originated in Ancient Egypt, but subsequently diffused across the whole world), the presence of, for example, agriculture and metal processing in both the Old and New Worlds would seem to indicate multiple independent innovation events. Perhaps the roots of this observation are twofold – one is the inherent creativity of the human species, the origins of which predate the dispersion of anatomically modern humans across the world, and secondly represent a generically human response to environmental challenges and opportunities. Although tool use is no longer seen as the unique defining characteristic of modern humans, it is probably still true to identify creativity of mind and an associated bodily capacity as a distinctive feature of humans.

The question of the sources of inspiration for human inventiveness has been extensively considered in the context of archaeology, as well as more broadly. The usual context of such a debate is the contrast between unique individual inspiration, apparently unrelated to any obvious precursor (usually manifested as a male inventor, either named or unnamed), or a more gradual and possibly collective response to a particular challenge, which may be incremental in nature. As with all such polarized debates, the truth in most cases is likely to be more hybrid and ambiguous, and to vary from place to place and time to time.

In differentiating between these two extremes of innovation, which we may paraphrase as spontaneous or evolutionary, the most common test applied would be to search for the presence of absence of identifiable antecedents. The efficacy of such an approach clearly depends on whether the search for an antecedent is sufficiently broadly based. To use a hypothetical and simplified example from literature, it would be misleading to assume that a particular idea expressed in a specific text written in, say, Latin had no precedent if the only other texts searched were those in Latin, to the neglect of possible antecedents in other languages such as Greek or Arabic. The extension of this to archaeological material culture becomes problematic. The example of the Antikythera mechanism given above shows that certain technologies can appear with no known antecedents (and, incidentally, shows how a single find can completely change our perceptions of the knowledge and skills of the past). How far should we look for possible technological precedents? For example, if we are interested in developments in metallurgy, should we only search for precedents in metal? The possibility of cross-craft fertilization would suggest that this is unwise, and the parallel technologies of glass-making and bronze production would suggest that such technology transfer is at least possible.

Although glass-making and bronze production have clear differences, they share one important property – both glass and bronze go through a liquid state during the production process, and this hugely affects the possibilities for human manipulation. It opens up the potential for the introduction of variable amounts of material to modify the properties (such as colour), but also the possibility of wholesale or partial recycling. A synchronicity of practice has already been observed in the use of compounds of antimony (Sb) in both glass and metal in the Roman period (Bray et al., in press). In glass, small amounts of antimony oxide (typically around 1 per cent Sb_2O_5) has the effect of countering the tinge of green introduced by excess iron entering the glass as an impurity, resulting in a truly colourless transparent glass. Iron and antimony act as a redox couple, with the antimony being reduced from Sb_2O_5 to its lowest oxidation state (Sb_2O_3) and the iron being oxidized from FeO to its highest state (Fe_2O_3). This has the effect of changing the colour caused by iron in a soda-lime-silica glass from green to a much weaker yellow colour, thus effectively decolorizing the glass (Pollard et al., 2017: 204–12). At higher concentration levels, the antimony combines with calcium to precipitate as calcium antimonate ($Ca_2Sb_2O_7$ or $Ca_2Sb_2O_6$), which acts as an opacifier. In their pioneering classification of the composition of archaeological glasses, Sayre and Smith (1961) identified a group which contained high levels of antimony, dating from the sixth century BCE to the fourth century CE. In the earlier part of this period it was widespread across Greece, Asia Minor and Persia, but during the Roman period its focus moved eastward.

The use of antimony in copper alloys has also been extensively studied. Small amounts of antimony – around 0.2 per cent – in copper alloy (80 per cent Cu, 10 per cent Sn, 10 per cent Pb) have been shown to increase the hardness of the alloy, although further additions show no further increase (Eggenschwiler, 1932). Although objects of pure antimony are rare, many bronzes from the Early Bronze Age onwards have been found to contain antimony up to several per cent (Gladstone, 1892). From the Bronze Age through to the Roman period in Europe, antimony is a common trace element in the copper alloys of many periods and places. However, it is almost always associated with other trace elements, notably arsenic, but also silver and nickel. A marked change is seen in the chemical compositions of assemblages of Roman copper alloys – a group of metals emerge in which antimony is the *only* trace element present in the alloy, although the alloying elements (tin, lead zinc) may also be present. This is unique in the history of British copper alloys, and, furthermore, a detailed study of the metals in Roman copper alloy coinage shows that it is a phenomenon which is widespread across the Empire (Bray et al., in press). From the reign of Nero (54 CE–68 CE) to that of Commodus (180 CE–192 CE), the copper coinage shows this distinctive antimony-only impurity pattern. Before this, from Augustus (27 BCE–14 CE) to some of Nero's issues, the coins are made of very pure copper, with very low levels of trace element impurities. From Commodus (180 CE–192 CE) to Probus (276 CE–282 CE), the coinage changes from unalloyed copper or brass (copper and zinc) to leaded bronze (copper with tin and lead), and the associated trace element pattern also changes to one containing both antimony and silver, although the antimony-only pattern also persists. The combination of silver and antimony probably represents a mixing of the antimony impurity from the copper with an input of silver associated with the added lead.

The metallurgical implication of this is that the early Imperial coinage (before Nero, *c*.54 CE) was made from very pure copper – probably smelted from a very pure source of copper ore, but possibly also reflecting a high degree of refining. Pure copper is, however, relatively soft, and therefore not suitable for a practical high-circulation coinage. The strike of the die could be poorly defined, and the coin would rapidly wear in circulation. The addition of a small percentage of antimony, as noted above, would increase the hardness of the coin, improving both the strike and the durability. But how was this addition achieved? It could be that a new source of copper was found which gave the desired composition, although sources of copper which contain only antimony as a trace impurity are rare, if they exist at all – no suitable candidate mining area has yet been identified. More likely, a small amount of antimony – from the coin evidence, up to 1 per cent by weight – was added to the refined copper. This is the point at which we turn towards the glass industry for inspiration. As noted above, similar small amounts of antimony added to green tinted glass can render the product completely transparent. Is it possible that the practice of adding small amounts of antimony was transferred from glassmaking to metal production? The timing is consistent, in the sense that although the use of antimony in glassmaking predates the Roman Imperial period, the vast expansion in glass production throughout the Empire would have greatly increased the demand for transparent glass by the first century CE.

Consistency of timing, especially if only approximate, is, of course, not sufficient to demonstrate a clear link between the two practices. Unfortunately, the contemporary written sources are silent on details such as this. It therefore has to remain speculation as to whether there is any relationship, until further possible synergies can be explored. Furthermore, to a modern mind, it might seem unlikely that a similar solution would be sought for two completely different problems in two distinct materials – a lack of transparency in glass, and a softness in copper alloy. What could have linked the two, to the Roman mind, might have been that both materials were thought of as suffering from a defect – possibly even perceived of as having an 'illness'.

This example prompts a new set of thoughts, and, importantly in this context, opens up the possibility of a new source of inspiration for technological change, which has yet to be fully explored, summarized as '*Medicine for the Material World*' – a connection between the pharmacological and the technological efficacy of particular minerals. Such a connection is not surprising or new, at least in a Chinese context, since Needham and Lu (1974: 14) suggested that the pharmaceutical use of inorganic drugs was one of the three roots of Chinese alchemy (the others being the pharmaceutical use of plants, and the metallurgical processes of making gold). In Chinese alchemy, from the beginning, there has always been an assumption that whatever worked as the 'philosopher's stone' in gold manufacture would also serve as the 'elixir of life' for humans (Needham and Lu, 1974: 11). This connection is generally less explicit in Western alchemy, but the thirteenth Century CE Oxford philosopher and alchemist Roger Bacon wrote in Chapter XII (on the Second Prerogative of Experimental Science) of his *Opus Majus*: 'For that medicine which would remove all the impurities and corruptions of a baser metal, so that it should become silver and purest gold, is thought by scientists to be able to remove the corruptions of the human body to such an extent that it would prolong life for many ages' (Burke, 1928: 627). Clearly Bacon saw the connection between alchemical transmutation and medical efficacy. Thus the link between the technological and medicinal applications of inorganic compounds is one which deserves further exploration, specifically in the context of drivers for technological innovation.

Technology exists in the material world, but the material world of previous generations would have looked very different to ours. In the West, our scientific belief system is now structured around, for all practical purposes, a Daltonian atomistic model of matter, existing within a mechanical Newtonian universe of forces and energy. The concept of the material world in the past would have varied over time, space and cultural identity, but would probably have included a wide range of mythical or supernatural beings with magical and other powers. In such a universe the boundary between this world and others would at least be semi-permeable, and the distinction between animate and inanimate was likely to be transgressive or irrelevant. If we suppose that in previous belief systems the material world conceptually merged with the animate world, and the human world in particular, then it follows that what was a suitable 'medicine' for human ailments might also be efficacious for 'diseases' in the material world.

This is not to reactivate the debate about vitalism, nor to engage with the biblical concepts of the soul. It is merely to argue that if we do not overly emphasise the difference between animate and inanimate objects, then it is not unreasonable to ask if concepts of 'medicine' can be transferred from humans to technological processes. Antimony presents an obvious candidate. As argued above, there are two (possibly related) examples of the use of antimony in technological processes, one involving glass and one copper.

A further example of the technological use of antimony is in the parting of gold from silver. Naturally occurring gold is often an alloy of gold and silver, called electrum, with perhaps up to 40 per cent silver. With the advent of the use of state-controlled gold coinage in Lydia in the sixth century BCE, it became important to be able to separate the gold from silver in order to guarantee the fineness of the coinage. The earliest method described to do this is called salt cementation, in which layers of argentiferous gold (electrum) sheets are sandwiched between layers of salt (NaCl) and brick dust in a sealed vessel. The chloride ions react with silver in the electrum to form insoluble silver chloride (AgCl) to leave pure gold. The silver chloride can be recovered and converted by smelting back to silver. This process is attested to from the sixth century BCE onwards (Craddock, 2000a). As an aside, it is striking that this process (the sandwiching of electrum and salt in a sealed vessel) is reminiscent of the traditional east Asian process of making pickled vegetables – layering vegetables and salt together in a sealed vessel. One is tempted to ask what is the relationship, if any, between these two technologies – which came first? It further reinforces the idea that technology does not exist divorced from the processes of everyday life.

Other salts can be used in the process, either in addition to NaCl or as a replacement for it, and of particular importance here is the use of antimony and stibnite (Sb_2S_3). The *Probierbüchlein* ('The little book on assaying'), written by an unknown German goldsmith or assayer around 1520 CE (Sisco and Smith, 1949), contains details of the use of antimony as an aid to the granulation of gold, which is an alternative to beating the gold into sheets before salt cementation. The recipes for this (Craddock, 2000b) give the amounts of antimony (with or without lead) to be added to gold. The *Probierbüchlein* also describes a later medieval alternative to the salt cementation process which uses sulphur, either provided as elemental sulphur, or more conveniently in the form of the antimony sulphide stibnite (Sb_2S_3). In this process the sulphur oxidizes the impurities in the finely divided gold to the sulphide species (Ag_2S, etc.), leaving the gold unaffected. The process works at a lower temperature than the salt cementation process, but appears to have been unknown in Antiquity. These processes were gradually replaced during the Renaissance with the increasing availability and purity of mineral acids, which will preferentially dissolve the silver from the gold. Nevertheless, the association between antimony and gold in these technological processes leads naturally to a discussion of the role of antimony in alchemical processes, discussed further below.

In historical terms, antimony (or its sulphide, stibnite Sb_2S_3) was extensively used in Ancient Egypt for black eye makeup (kohl) (although both lead and antimony sulphides were used). Perhaps relatedly, stibnite was also used as a medicine in Ancient Egypt. Medical papyri dating from at least 1550 BCE (the Hearst and Ebers papyri: Nunn, 1996) attest to the use of stibnite as a cure for headache and conjunctivitis, but not as an emetic (Kamal, 1926). By the mid eighteenth century in Europe, however, antimony is described primarily as an emetic. The recipe given by Huxham (1756) recommends the preparation of 'Essentia, or vinum Antimonii' as follows: '*Let one ounce of well prepared Glass of Antimony, powdered, be infused, cold, in 24 ounces of sound Madeira wine for 10 or 12 days, shaking it sometimes. Let it settle for a day or two, then decant the Wine, and filter it through whitish-brown paper, and keep it in a glass-bottle, well stopped*'. A dose of between thirty to eighty drops for adults would then act as a very effective emetic purge.

The most significant pre-modern references to antimony come, however, in the alchemical literature, and most specifically in the writings of Basil Valentine. Like many alchemical writers, the very existence of a single person called Basil Valentine is disputed. Conventionally he is identified as a Benedictine monk at the Priory of Erfurt in central Germany, and dated to the fifteenth century, but most likely his writings are provided by others, including, but perhaps not exclusively, Johann Thölde, a German salt manufacturer active during the late sixteenth and early seventeenth century (Pierce, 1898). The most significant work of Basil Valentine is translated into English as *The Triumphal Chariot of Antimony*, which first appeared in Amsterdam in 1604 (Waite, 1893).

This work has multiple significance in the present context. The following passage emphasizes the pervasiveness of the 'operative and vital spirit', at least as perceived by the late medieval *Magisterium*:

> *But to return to the science of Antimony. You should know that all things contain operative and vital spirits, which derive their substance and nourishment from their bodies; nor are the elements themselves without these spirits, whether good or evil. Men and animals have within them an operative and vitalizing spirit, and if it forsakes them, nothing but a dead body is left. Herbs and trees have spirits of health, else no Art could turn them to medicinal uses. In the same way, minerals and metals possess vitalizing spirits, which constitute their whole strength and goodness: for what has no spirit has no life, or vitalizing power. Know that in Antimony also there is a spirit which is its strength, which also pervades it invisibly, as the magnetic property pervades the magnet.* (Waite, 1893: 30)

This quote illustrates two points in the context of this volume. The observation that minerals and metals 'possess vitalizing spirits' supports the contention that there was perceived to be a continuum between the animate and inanimate world, and encourages the thought that materials used as medicine for humans might also have been seen as suitable 'medicine' for the ills of the material world. Secondly, the focus on antimony as a medicine and a technological additive is, in this context, purely illustrative of what we suggest could be a much wider pattern. Other materials, such as the use of zinc oxide ('calamine') as a medicine to treat skin diseases and diseases of the eye (Pooley, 1693), as well as its role in the production of brass (Povey, 1693), are so far less well researched in terms of any possible synergies. Nevertheless, we propose that transfer of agents from *materia medica* to the world of technological innovation should be added to the list of potential drivers for technological change. It is worth observing that, in most *materia medica* from the ancient world, the vast majority of the agents listed are usually biological – derived from plants or animals – rather than mineralogical. Whilst not dismissing the possibility that such agents could have been used for some perceived purpose in technological processes, it is pertinent to note that any trace of their use is unlikely to have survived if the process involved heating or chemical processing. Thus any evidence for such activities might be difficult to come by. In other words, if a medically active plant such as ginseng was perceived as having some import-ant action in the production of glass or metal, we would probably not be able to know about it unless its use was recorded in some literary source. We do know from some later Islamic sources (e.g., Matin and Pollard, 2015) that gums were sometimes used in the production of glass frit and raw pigments, so we should not be blind to the role of organic materials in technological processes, but it currently provides a greater analytical challenge than the study of inorganic agents.

The perceived link between the material and the human world in the past is perhaps illustrated by the concept of animism, as defined by Tylor (1871). Although we would not now wish to engage with Tylor's perspective of animism as the spirituality of 'the lower races' (indeed, a modern perspective might see these 'savages' as being more ecologically enlightened than the 'higher races'), but his definition of animism as 'first, concerning souls of individual creatures, capable of continued existence after the death or destruc-tion of the body; second, concerning other spirits, upward to the rank of powerful deities' (Tylor, 1871: Vol. 1, p. 426), is perhaps helpful, especially the second part. In his opinion, animism 'constitutes . . . an ancient and world-wide philosophy' (Tylor, 1871: Vol. 1, p. 427). Without subscribing to the nineteenth century perceptions of indigenous cultures, and acknowledging the dangers of projecting modern anthropological observations back into earlier times, it seems reasonable to accept that the distinction between the animate and inanimate world may have been much more fluid than they are now, at least in some places and at some times. More explicitly, after considering the souls of animals and plants, Tylor discusses the belief in the souls of objects, noting that such beliefs are particularly strong amongst the Algonquin of North America, the islanders of the Fiji group and the Karens of Burma. He notes (Tylor, 1871: Vol. 1, p. 479) that the Algonquin peoples equated the shadow with the soul, and therefore believed that all inanimate objects must also possess a soul. The Fijians believed that 'If an axe or a chisel is worn out or broken, away flies its soul for the service of the Gods'. Moreover, Tylor sees such ideas transitioning into Greek philosophy, citing Democritus in the fifth century BCE, who stated that perception is the result of objects throwing off images of themselves into the surrounding air, which enter a recipient soul to be seen. This idea is subsequently developed by Lucretius and the Epicureans to explain both the process of cognition but also to account for apparitions. Tylor concludes: 'Such are the debts which civilized philosophy owes to primitive animism' (Tylor, 1871: Vol. 1, p. 498). For many years the colonialist framework of Tylor's work meant that the concept of animism was not widely considered, but more recently the term has been revived to describe the ways in which humans engage with their non-human neighbours (e.g., animals, plants, objects, rocks, clouds: Harvey, 2005).

Further, in an animistic world the traditional tribal shaman operates as an intermediary between the human community and the wider non-human world (Abram, 1996: 14). Human ailments (as well as many other detrimental factors such as drought, famine, etc.) are attributed to an imbalance between the human and non-human world, and shamanic healers operate by bringing these factors back into balance. It is no great extension to consider that similar shamanic interventions could be brought to bear on defects in the material world, such as a lack of transparency in glass, or the softness of pure copper. This seems to provide sufficient encouragement to pursue the idea that, since animate and inanimate were related in the past, medicines for the one could have application for the other.

More scientific approaches have often seen technological progress to be driven by a classical 'push–pull' mechanism. The 'push' comes from factors such as the need to adapt to changing environments, or to utilize natural resources more efficiently to sustain larger populations, or to compete with some neighbouring group who may have achieved some technological advantage. 'Push' in this sense is almost entirely a responsive force. The 'pull' takes the form of human ingenuity and creativity, and therefore can be more proactive (although a responsive mode may still require a spark of creativity). Somebody, somewhere, sees a better way of doing something, or an advantage in using a particular object as a tool, and 'invents' a new process. Another way of looking at this might be to think of 'push' being a responsive mode in which some specific objective was intended, whereas 'pull' is created by a spontaneous event, observation or thought which somebody realizes can be turned to advantage. Understanding the balance between these forces of push and pull is one of the major challenges in explaining the course of human development. If 'push' predominates, then one might expect human societies in different parts of the world, and at different times, to respond to the same set of stimuli in the same way, and this gives rise to a model of multiple independent invention of objects or processes. If 'pull' predominates, then we may be witness to a single event of creative genius, which is then somehow communicated far and wide – a more diffusionist model for technological development. We might now see push and pull differently, in the sense that new materials and forms operate a pull, best seen as a space of possibility into which people can expand and become reskilled within. Necessity may be the mother of invention, but what is necessary to one group might seem irrelevant or superfluous to another.

Technology Transfer

Whatever the driver for technological innovation, there also has to be a process by which technical know-how is transferred from person to person or group to group, otherwise a particular innovation, however brilliant or useful, would die out within a generation. Moreover, one can envisage a scenario whereby an invention, no matter how significant, if it is not successfully transferred either geographically (*horizontal transmission*) or through the generations (*vertical transmission*), will disappear, as we shall consider below.

It would seem self-evident that two factors are important here – one is the ease by which person-to-person contact can facilitate the transfer of technological know-how (Kuijpers, 2018), and the second is the influence of population density, or connectivity, of the community within which the invention is being transferred. The learning of manual procedures and craft skills is something which, in modern society at least, is best done by face-to-face contact with an exponent of the procedure, and learning experientially. It is widely assumed that the transmission of skills in the past has been based on some form of apprenticeship, perhaps involving generational transmission within a family or group, or possibly through some form of commercial apprenticeship. The former is likely to give rise to a particular family or group acquiring a reputation for a particular expertise, leading perhaps to specialization and closed groups of such specialists.

Transmission can also be done through spoken language – somebody describing a process to another person who may have enough experience in related processes to be able to do it from this description (or, perhaps, using spoken language in addition to a physical demonstration to explain the intricacies of a procedure, or the rationale behind an action). It can also be done through the written word, perhaps in combination with sketches (but how many people can really assemble flat pack furniture?). Thus one suspects that the development of linguistic ability is likely to have been a significant factor in the early phase of human technological evolution, whereas the degree to which the invention of writing may have facilitated the transmission of technological innovation, until the age of mass communication via printed text, may have been minimal. The role of language and written communication in stimulating a market for particular goods, such as Marco Polo's descriptions of the wonders of Kubilai Khan's court (Ricci, 1931), may, however, have been more significant, and may have led to technological experimentation to reproduce or imitate such goods.

Another key factor in technology transmission for state level societies is the organization of artisans, and the relationship between artisans and the elite (Brysbaert and Gorgues, 2017). During the Bronze and Iron Ages of the Ancient Near East, and also in the Greek and Hellenistic world, the dominant social organization was the city state, controlled by a central Palace economy. This region is broadly credited with the earliest practice of settled agriculture, the innovation of writing systems (initially largely as an accounting mechanism for agricultural products), the invention of the potter's wheel, as well as the origins of the city-state, and often an associated religious system. Such a dispersed system of independent city states led to an ever-changing network of alliances (often based on marriage) and enmities, warfare and empires, and also intricate and deeply embedded systems of trade and exchange. Such systems held sway in this area from the Neolithic (*c.* sixth millennium BCE) until the Iron Age (first millennium BCE), when large scale empires (perhaps beginning with that of Alexander the Great in the fourth century BCE) swept away the power of independent city-states.

The functioning of some of the palaces at the heart of the city-state during the Bronze Age has been partially revealed through the archaeological recovery of the written palace records. In Mesopotamia and Assyria these take the form of baked clay tablets inscribed with cuneiform text. A common format for these palace or temple records is the recording of the issue of raw materials from the palace or temple stores, and the receipt of the required finished goods (Moorey, 1994: 14). The most significant assemblage of administrative archives comes from the III Dynasty of Ur, dating to the end of the third millennium BCE (Neumann, 1987). This archive, recovered by Leonard Woolley, was used by

Limet (1960) in his study of the metalworking workshop, but is also interesting because it reveals the close working relationship between different groups of workers. Eight types of worker are listed – blacksmiths (interesting here because it predates the widespread use of iron!), carpenters, felters, goldsmiths, leatherworkers, metalworkers, reed workers, and stonecutters.

Slightly later, the Old Babylonian records (*c.*2000 BCE–1600 BCE) from the Palace of Mari, whilst emphasizing the importance of silver, also refer to the production of bronze. One tablet, from Zimri-Lim, King of Mari from approximately 1775 to 1761 BCE, to Mukannishum, the bronze smith, instructs him to:

> *As soon as you have read this letter, have made 50 bronze arrow-(heads) of 40 g weight each, 50 arrow-(heads) of 24 g weight each, 100 arrow-(heads) of 16 g weight each, and 200 arrow-(heads) of 8 g weight each. Make it a priority, so that it is finished quickly. It looks as if the siege of Andarik may be prolonged, and that is why I am writing to you for those arrows.* (Dalley, 1984: 63)

From an overview of these records, some common features of Palatial organization emerge. It is clear that the Palace controlled the supply of copper and other metals, as well as selected other goods (often textiles, perfumes, and oils). Since most Palaces are usually located in regions poor in metallic raw materials, the supply of metals was secured from the metal production regions by trade using the other goods controlled by the palace – often high quality textiles. The palace stored the raw metal, and supplied it to craftsmen when particular work was commissioned. Some records say that the metal was weighed when it was given out, and the finished goods weighed on delivery, to prevent fraud. Crucially, it is usually not clear from these written records whether the craftsmen were palace employees, temple employees, independent craftsmen, or slaves. Exceptionally, Nakassis (2013: 74), using a prosopographical approach to the names from the records of Pylos in Greece *c.*1200 BCE, concluded that 'significant numbers of smiths and herders are individuals tasked with multiple responsibilities by the palatial authority', suggesting that these smiths were part-time metal producers, who probably worked independently. This analysis also showed that two-thirds of the 263 named smiths received bronze or copper (but in relatively small amounts – average 3.5 kg per smith per year) from the palace to be worked into finished products, whereas one-third did not. This, and also the Babylonian accounts, leads to the suggestion of the existence of itinerant individuals or workshops, moving from palace to palace. Although the records are primarily interested in the control of Palace supplies, it is sometimes suggested that it was also common for private (i.e., non-Palatial) customers to commission work from the same craftsmen, and also to provide them with the necessary raw materials for metal production.

In terms of technology transfer, it is clear that the movement of skilled craftspeople could provide an important vector, whether it is through itinerant workers, or palace workers being given to other kingdoms as part of the development of an alliance (Burford, 1972). When this is added to evidence from other sources, it is clear that skilled artisans were in and of themselves an important economic resource. It is said, for example, that Chinggis Khan, first Great Khan of the Mongol Empire, despite a reputation for ruthlessness in his treatment of enemies who opposed him, often spared the conquered crafts-people and relocated them to his capital at Karakorum in Mongolia. For example, Guzman (2010: 123), noted that 'it was the common Mongol practice to spare skilled craftsmen from massacre, to enslave needed workers, and to grant safe-conduct to merchants as well as to envoys and ambassadors'. Such mass movements of artisans, voluntarily or otherwise, must have provided a significant vector for technological communication.

A key element, implicitly or explicitly, within more scientific approaches to technological diffusion has been demography. Although there are many examples of particular technologies being 'lost' as a result of social change (e.g., the loss of wheel-thrown pots in the post-Roman period of Britain, the switch away from ceramics in later British Viking contexts as a result of the use of steatite to make vessels, or the loss of writing when the Mycenaean palatial economies ceased to exist), some studies of communities who have lost tech-nologies have shown that population size is an important factor. The prime example of this are native Tasmanians, who, after Tasmania became discon-nected from continental Australia about 8,000 years ago, gradually lost the skills required even for fishing and making clothing. Using a mathematical model which combines the efficiency of person-to-person transmission of skills, and the numbers of people on the island, Henrich (2004) has shown that effective population size is the most likely predictor of this loss of technology. Effective population size is not necessarily simply the number of people in the local or regional group – it must take into account the network of contacts at various levels experienced by these groups – hence the term connectivity rather than straightforward demography.

Reversing this argument, one might postulate a significant relationship between the effective size of the population pool and the likelihood that a particular invention or process can be sustainably propagated. Essentially such a model would suggest that technological complexity (taken here to mean the number of different active technologies) is positively correlated with effect-ive population size. This would then predict that increasing technological complexity is an inevitable consequence of growing population size, and might even explain the apparently common sequence of technological evolution seen throughout large parts of the world. Perhaps this is population determinism replacing technological determinism, for it is commonly conceived that technological advancement is the force which allows populations to grow. There are, of course, great dangers in adopting a single explanatory model for a process as complex as the evolution of material culture, and it is inevitable that multiple parameters will be necessary to explain the intricate features seen in the technological evolution of human society. It does, however, potentially challenge the notion that human cognitive ability has been the rate-controlling step in technological evolution. Is it possible that cognitive ability has been unchanged for many tens of thousands of years, if not longer, but that population connectivity has been the controlling factor in determining the rate of technological change?

Extrapolating this idea in a different direction, we might postulate the following scenario. In the unlikely event that metal smelting had been invented by early anatomically modern humans in East Africa 50,000 years ago, but not transferred for more than a generation or two, nor spread geographically over a large area because of the relatively low population density, then it would have disappeared from the archaeological record. In fact, given the partial nature of that record, the chances are that it would never be found at all – or, worse still, because it is an 'unexpected' find in a particular place or time, if found, it would be dismissed as an anomaly or error. This gives rise to what we might call a 'flickering candle' model for early technological innovation – developments may be made which splutter briefly, but are extinguished and disappear, and only if a 'critical mass' of people capable of carrying out that process or utilizing that tool is reached does the idea become sustainable. This condition may or may not be related to *total* population size, but a large population is *more likely* to give rise to such a condition. A technology is then established which will last as long as there is a need for that particular action, or until it is replaced by some other way of doing it. One is left with the question of how many times might a particular technological innovation have been 'invented', such as the smelting of the green mineral malachite ($Cu_2CO_3(OH)_2$) to produce metallic copper, relatively easily achieved on an open fire, before the sustainable 'invention' and spread of copper metallurgy.

In fact, there is a vast modern literature on 'diffusion research' – the way in which innovations are diffused through society – not to be confused with the archaeological concept of diffusionism, which can be brought to bear on this question. This now links into the modelling of complexity. Such research has been at the heart of social science studies of, for example, how knowledge about HIV protection is communicated through society, or how a new product may be marketed to consumers. A leading proponent of this research was Everett

Rogers (1931–2004), who has broken down the process of innovation diffusion into four stages, each of which is susceptible to further analysis (Rogers, 2003):

- Innovation,
- communication channels,
- time, and
- social systems.

In this context, *Innovation* is defined as an idea, practice, or object perceived as new by an individual or group (Rogers, 2003). Most technological innovations consist of two components, referred to in modern terminology as *hardware* (a tool which embodies the technology as a material object), and the associated *software* (the knowledge base necessary for the use of that tool). Innovations are perceived to have five characteristics, which can be combined to determine the rate of adoption, if successful, or to explain why a technology was not adopted:

- *relative advantage* (over preceding or competing technologies, but which is not restricted to an economic or technological definition – it may well include prestige),
- *compatibility* with existing knowledge bases,
- *complexity* (the perceived difficulty of use and/or understanding),
- *trialability* (the ease with which an innovation may be tested against existing methods),
- *observability* (the degree to which an improvement can be seen).

An additional dimension to innovation is *re-invention*, which in this context implies the extent to which an innovation is used by the adopting person or community for a purpose other than that for which it was intended. Not specifically discussed by Rogers is a concept which we might term *co-invention*, or perhaps *consequent invention* – a series of related or enabling technologies, such as metalled roads, which were unnecessary before the widespread use of motor vehicles, but whose invention greatly enhanced the functionality of motor cars once they had been invented. More generally, Rogers addresses this interrelationship with the idea of *technology clusters*, which he defines as 'one or more indistinguishable elements of technology that are perceived as being closely related'. This is clearly an extremely significant concept in the archaeological context, where we routinely talk about concepts such as 'the Neolithic package', which might include agriculture, pottery, and, in Eurasia, the Indo-European languages. In archaeology, the term technology cluster is perhaps contained within the concept of a techno-complex, which is used to define a characteristic assemblage of material objects, which in turn may define an archaeological culture, but it is clearly not synonymous.

The *communication channel* is the means by which information about an innovation is communicated from one individual to another. In modern times, this often involves the mass media, or, increasingly, social media, but historically would have been largely limited to person-to-person contact. Interestingly, in modern studies it has been shown that although the presence of mass media can affect the rate at which innovations are diffused, the overall characteristics are unchanged in person-to-person contact situations. Rogers distinguishes between *heterophilic* and *homophilic* communication, where the belief systems, education levels and socio-economic status, and so forth, of the participants are, respectively, either different or the same. In general, homophilic transmission is more effective – heterophilic transmission often requires the consent of one or more *opinion formers* in the system, who may be of higher status, and who signify their approval by adopting the innovation. An important concept here is that of the *communication network* which consists of interconnected individuals between whom information may flow. Within any communication network there will be a *critical mass*, which is defined as the number of adopters necessary in the network to ensure that adoption becomes self-sustaining. Not all adopters, however, are necessarily equal – a small number of opinion formers (fewer than the critical mass) may catalyse the system into becoming self-sustaining. These concepts clearly link to the above discussion of population size and connectivity, and strengthens the idea that critical mass is a central concept in the sustainability of technological innovation in antiquity.

In this context, *time* means the time taken for an innovation to diffuse through the system. One of the principal findings of this research is that the rate of uptake of an innovation, when plotted as number of participants over time, forms a characteristic S-shaped curve (an ogival cumulative distribution function, being the integral of a normal distribution). In diffusion research, it has become common to divide this curve into sections, denoting *innovators* (c. 2.5 per cent of the total population who adopt the innovation), *early adopters* (13.5 per cent), *early majority* (34 per cent), *late majority* (34 per cent) and *laggards* (16 per cent) (Figure 3).

The *social system*, according to Rogers, is 'a set of interrelated units that are engaged in joint problem solving to accomplish a common goal'. In mathematical terms, the social system defines the universe through which the innovation is deemed to diffuse. It might be all the villagers in a particular village, or a collection of villages in a particular region, or all adult males in a particular city, or all the consumers in Europe, depending on the nature of the study. It is the correct definition of this social system which is vitally important in archaeology, and needs careful consideration. In constructing these models, we should perhaps distinguish between *producers* and *consumers* – producers are those

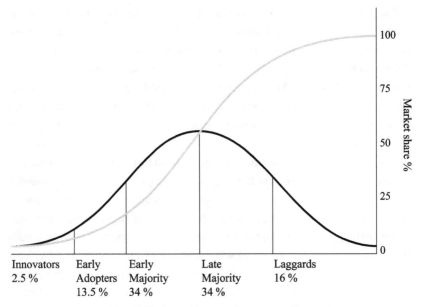

Innovators	Early	Early	Late	Laggards
2.5 %	Adopters	Majority	Majority	16 %
	13.5 %	34 %	34 %	

Figure 3 The diffusion of innovations according to Rogers

who are capable of manufacturing an object (pottery, metal), but we may also need to further distinguish between specialized craftspeople and household level producers. Consumers may consist of the entire population, or some subset of it, such as elite households, or farm workers.

Such a way of conceiving of society is useful when attempting to develop mathematical models concerning the movement of ideas, materials or people. However, the definition of a social system as a problem-solving unit will seem very partial to many, leaving out most of the things that make us most interesting as human beings. Such an approach is strong in shining a bright light on areas of innovation and change, but leaves other things in shadow, and also lacks a feedback system between material objects and humans. Given archaeological approaches which stress entanglement – within and between social systems, but also between humans and material culture – we might also want to see that the group is made up of both people and things, where both the human and the non-humans can act as facilitators or inhibitors of communication and cohesion.

Kim (2001) has looked at the different rates of adoption of iron into Bronze Age societies in Denmark (slow) and southern Korea (rapid), arguing that the differing rates in the two cases can best be explained by the differing natures of the two economies – Denmark having a more subsistence economy, and Korea being a more prestige economy (in which symbolism and ideology are used to shape social relations). In the prestige economy, the elites see an immediate role for iron in the production and distribution of prestige goods, leading to a rapid adoption of iron. Furthermore, he points out that the *'value laden assumption that iron replaced bronze because of its qualitative superiority over bronze'* is incorrect. In neither the prestige nor the subsistence economy did iron directly replace bronze – *'iron competed with stone as a primary material for subsistence production, and what really replaced bronze, the source of prestige-authoritarian power in both Bronze Ages, was a heavy dependence on administrative power and on systematic agricultural surplus appropriation'*. This is an important observation, even if not necessarily universally applicable, because it exposes one of the 'presentist' assumptions (Killick, 2001) made by many archaeologists – because bronze and iron are both metals, and to us all metals have broadly similar physical properties, then they must have fulfilled equivalent roles in their respective societies. Iron must therefore have supplanted bronze in all of its functions. Kim, amongst many others, has shown that this need not be the case.

Subsequent work has offered us the possibility of elaborating on the idea of the social system as defined by Rogers. This uses the concept of *social networks*, and in particular the idea of the *scale-free network* proposed by Barabási and Albert (1999) and Barabási (2002). A scale-free network is one which cannot be characterized by an average number of connections – it has a large number of nodes with few connections, but a small number of highly connected nodes. If the number of nodes with a given number of links is plotted as a function of the number of links, then the result looks like an exponential decay curve. The analogy used by Barabási to illustrate a scale-free network is a U.S. airline map, showing a large number of airports with only a few connections, but a small number of highly connected 'hubs'. In contrast, a so-called 'random' network is one such as the highway network into U.S. cities – some have only a few roads in, whereas others have more, but none have an extremely high number. Typically, most cities have about the same number of highway connections and therefore it is feasible to think of characterizing the network with an average number of connections. Barabási has pointed out that scale-free networks are a good model for Rogers' social systems, and that the hubs are effectively the 'opinion formers' in these social networks – the compliance of whom is critical to the effective diffusion of innovation.

It is remarkable to see how unusual it is for such analyses to be attempted in the mainstream of archaeological research. In a citation survey of Rogers' influential book *Diffusion of Innovations*, first published in 1962, using Web of Knowledge on 2 December 2020 (imperfect though this is for archaeological publications), one finds that of the more than 30,500 recorded citations of the several editions of his book, only 64 are categorized as being in the archaeological journal literature, compared with 77 in history, 176 in anthropology and

343 in geography. The majority of citations (more than 8,000) are, perhaps unsurprisingly, in management and business. Interestingly, however, of the 64 citations in archaeology, 25 are dated to between 2018 to 2020, suggesting that interest in these ideas is growing.

Barabási's concept of scale-free networks has had even less penetration, with perhaps the most successful work being done by Bentley (Bentley and Maschner, 2001; Bentley and Shennan, 2003), although one 'adopter' (Knappett, 2006) has made the suggestion that such networks should include non-human as well as human actors, an idea which echoes the views mentioned above. Overall, however, these ideas seem so far to have found little currency in archaeology, particularly amongst the more technologically focussed practitioners. And yet, to quote a reviewer of the first edition of Rogers' book (Bick, 1963): *'For the anthropologist, this book is an implicit criticism of the whole field on a number of levels. Perhaps the most devastating and yet least surprising criticism is also the most explicit: "the anthropology field is completely unaware that any other tradition on the diffusion of innovation exists."'* Gradually, this criticism, which could equally have been targeted at archaeology, and perhaps even more specifically at some of the histories of technology, is being addressed.

Technological Choice and 'Intentionality'

One of the most significant changes in the way in which archaeologists have approached technological studies of the material record in recent years has been the adoption of the concept of technological choice – incorporating the *chaîne opératoire* of Leroi-Gourhan (1964, 1965, 1993), deriving inspiration from the work of Mauss. The *chaîne opératoire* is the sequence of acts which link together to transform raw materials into objects – an idea which can be generalized to consider the life cycle of an object from manufacture through distribution and use to discard (and if necessary beyond, to burial and recovery). The starting point for this connection is the observation made by Kingery (1996), which he termed the 'materials science paradigm', which says that the artefact structure and composition are a direct consequence of the choices made by the potter, in terms of raw material selection and processing. In effect, the choices made during manufacture and use are encoded in the observed composition and structure of the finished object.

Sillar and Tite (2000) identify the following five 'areas of choice' within any ancient technology:

- raw material selection (to which we would add processing),
- tools used to shape the raw materials,
- source of energy to transform the raw materials and power any tools used,

- techniques used to orchestrate the raw materials, tools, and energy to achieve a particular goal, and
- the sequence (the *chaîne opératoire*) in which these acts are linked together to transform raw material into finished product.

This *chaîne opératoire* approach has been used to study the selection of raw materials (clays and temper), the manufacturing technology (type of construction method used), the firing process and the finishing processes in pottery manufacture. At each point, the materials science properties are considered alongside the practical and aesthetic choices made by the potter. In many cases, the physical properties are seen to be a significant component in this choice. For example, the type of firing (typically the choice being an open bonfire vs. an updraft kiln) is said to be dictated by the type of fabric being made – coarse fabrics being more porous and capable of withstanding the rapid heating (and consequent rapid evolution of water vapour) typical of a bonfire, whereas fine fabrics require the slower, more controlled, heating provided by a kiln. Whilst this is a neat technical explanation, and a clear example of the need to match the process to the product, it is perhaps not quite so clear in which direction the choice is being made – does the nature of the product dictate the required firing methodology, or is the availability (or otherwise) of the kiln dictating the nature of the product? Perhaps even more critically, one of the significant contributions of some technological studies of ceramic production has been the identification of what sort of clay was required to produce a particular type of ceramic. Whilst it is perfectly legitimate to observe that some types of ceramic such as high-gloss Roman Terra Sigillata (samian) are best produced using a calcareous clay, this can only be inferred as a choice if we know the distribution of potential clay sources, and can show that calcareous clays were preferentially selected over other *available* sources of clay. If this is the case, then we might infer deliberate choice of raw material – but we may again pose the question 'is this raw material dictating product, or does the desired product dictate the choice of raw material?' (Figure 4). None of this should be taken to imply that we believe that ancient potters did not know what they were doing – this is clearly refuted by almost every technological analysis of pottery ever carried out – but it perhaps illustrates a limitation on the degree to which technological choices can be inferred from materials properties, in the absence of a great deal of other information.

These are perhaps examples of the sort of 'linear analysis' which Sillar and Tite (2000: 4) warn against:

> *Nonetheless, this analysis will not be sufficient if it is confined to a linear analysis of how a particular object was made. It is only through a consideration of the overall context that affects the availability of resources*

Figure 4 Chinese potters cutting clay (and being brought tea). (Wellcome Collection nineteenth century ink drawing)

as well as the valuation of alternative techniques that we will be able to explain why particular technological choices were made and what material and social effects they had. This overall context spans the environmental and technological constraints, the economic and subsistence base, the social and political organization, and the ideology or belief systems of the people making the choices.

One very valuable recent development has been the application of organic chemistry analytical techniques to ceramics which has enabled the *chaîne opératoire* approach to be extended into life cycle analysis, by allowing the use of the vessel to be examined via the organic remains preserved in or on the vessel. Analogous to this has been the physical use-wear analysis of tools and other objects such as jewellery – initially of stone tools, but more recently extended to cover bone objects and metals. Some progress has also been made in applying biochemical analysis to residues on stone and other tools – initially (and controversially) blood residues on stone tools, but more recently carbohydrate residues from plant processing. These approaches have enabled function to be determined from use residues rather than inferred from form and context, and as such are yet another tool in identifying the choices made, but this time during the useful life of the object. It is sometimes also possible to distinguish between primary and secondary (or subsequent) use, such as the reuse of broken Roman transport amphorae as pissoirs in Roman buildings.

One further approach to using technological analysis of objects to understand more about the influence of social, cultural and ideological factors on ancient technological processes has been the concept of technological style, introduced by Lechtman (1977). In essence, technological style is a combination of factors which limit or guide the choices made by a craftsperson, to reflect the current norms of expectation. Similar ideas were developed within the French anthropological tradition by Lemonnier (1986) in an 'attempt to relate techniques, in their most material aspects, directly to the characteristics of the societies which developed them'. Lemonnier, however, goes much further than this. He chastises anthropologists interested in material culture for ignoring technological processes at the expense of collecting artefacts (resulting in museums full of 'lifeless objects'). Moreover, he emphasizes that individual technological processes (such as weaving a basket) cannot be studied in isolation from all of the other processes carried out by that community, since they are all related and interlinked. One might be tempted, after reading Lemonnier, to conclude that archaeologists have a hopeless task in studying the material culture of vanished societies, given these necessities! However, archaeology is different to anthropology, in that almost all we have to work with is material culture, and so we must devise approaches which allow us to infer social structures and practices from these 'lifeless objects' to the best of our abilities. And yet there are lessons to be learned from Lemmonier's views – not least that in archaeology there is an overwhelming tradition of studying different materials separately. The 'specialist syndrome', whereby excavated objects of metal are sent to one person for description and analysis, those of glass to another, and ceramics to yet another, does not facilitate the sort of integrated consideration of technical systems as advocated by Lemonnier. Historians of ancient technologies therefore face a huge challenge in attempting to integrate the information obtained from the material remnants of many technological processes into one coherent social picture.

A major assumption in the *chaîne opératoire* process is that the choices made by the artisan are conscious and deliberate – that clay is sourced from location A rather than location B, or that metal is smelted from ore obtained at mine C rather than D. If they are not conscious choices, then the process is uninformative, in that it reveals a sequence of random steps. How do we distinguish between what is conscious and deliberate, and what is a random decision? Here we term this understanding the 'intentionality' of the artisan – what did s/he know and think about the process, and why did they take particular decisions? An important and much-debated example of this question in the context of the early stages of copper alloying is the differentiation, if it really exists, between 'accidental' and 'deliberate' alloying.

In modern materials science, an alloy is defined as a mixture of metals designed to improve the physical, mechanical or visual properties of the material. Roberts et al. (2009) define intentional alloying in an archaeological context as the 'deliberate choices made in the production process, whether in the selection of ores or the mixing of metals'. This is clearly reasonable, since an alloy (such as bronze, made from a majority of copper and a minority of tin) could in principal be made either by directly mixing together metallic copper and tin, or by blending ores containing both copper and tin prior to smelting (co-smelting). Variations on these two mechanisms could include partially replacing either the copper or tin in the direct mixing process with a recycled metal containing tin, or, in the co-smelting model, by using a naturally occurring mixed ore rather than an artificial mixture. The point here is that it is difficult to know without the evidence of information directly from the mind of the artisan what was known or believed about the raw materials and what was being controlled in the process. For example, the same alloy could be achieved by following several very different mental paths. In one, for example, the ores to be co-smelted could be deliberately sourced from a particular mine or region, because experience had shown that the result would be suitable for a particular purpose. In another, the ores could be selected not by geographical source but on the basis of colour, texture, or smell, since experience would have shown that a particular combination gave a particular product (Pollard et al., 2018: 126–33). A third process might involve melting copper and adding either a particular 'earth', or a specific metal or alloy, to give a product with the desired properties.

There is an element of 'intentionality' or deliberate selection in all of these process, but the actual chemistry might neither be understood or controlled, and could therefore be termed (by us) as 'accidental'. Clearly, the relationship between the geographical location of an ore, the geological make-up of the ore and the decisions taken during processing can combine to render the process somewhat opaque to our mind, whereas it would have been very clear to the artisans. It might therefore be better to say that the terms 'deliberate' and 'accidental' refer more to our understanding rather than applying to the original intentionality of the artisan, since in her or his mind the rationale may have been abundantly clear. We must acknowledge, of course, that the original rationale would have been based on their perception of the material world, not ours, and could well have included mythical or magical components. In the light of this, it seems unhelpful to adopt a system which defines one particular process as 'deliberate', but some others not. It might be overstating the case, but perhaps it is appropriate to regard all alloys as the product of a deliberate process, and, by extension, to regard all technological processes as deliberate in one way or another.

This perhaps begs the question about the nature and status of experimentation in the process of technological change. If all technological processes were deliberate in one way or another, there is then little scope for change, other than by specific experimentation, or as a result of a genuine accident. The traditional explanation for the discovery of glass-making as given by Pliny would fall into this latter category, if it were true. In Book 36 of his Natural History, Pliny the Elder writes:

> *In Syria there is a region known as Phœnice, adjoining to Judœa, and enclosing, between the lower ridges of Mount Carmelus, a marshy district known by the name of Cendebia. In this district, it is supposed, rises the river Belus, which, after a course of five miles, empties itself into the sea near the colony of Ptolemaïs...... The story is, that a ship, laden with nitre, being moored upon this spot, the merchants, while preparing their repast upon the sea-shore, finding no stones at hand for supporting their cauldrons, employed for the purpose some lumps of nitre which they had taken from the vessel. Upon its being subjected to the action of the fire, in combination with the sand of the sea-shore, they beheld transparent streams flowing forth of a liquid hitherto unknown: this, it is said, was the origin of glass.*
>
> (Bostock and Riley, 1857: Vol. 6, Book 36, Chapter 65).

Nitre is now generally translated as natural soda, that is, the mineral natron.

It seems likely that there has to be a stage of experimentation in technological processes, such as experimental alloying, for example, mixing two ores in a co-smelt without knowing what the particular outcome would be. This involves a deliberate action but the resultant properties of the alloy would be unpredictable from the experience of the artisans. It suggests a process in which an experiment is undertaken, and the efficacy of the process judged *post-hoc* by evaluating the usefulness of the product. The same idea could equally be applied to the adventitious product of a process which 'went wrong', but nevertheless produced a useful product, leading to a change in the process, if the source of the original 'error' could be identified and replicated. How long such an 'experimental phase' may have lasted, whether it occurred once or many times in different places, and what are the chances of identifying such a phase in the archaeological record, remain open questions.

Final Thoughts

Technologies involve the embodiment of magic and wonder. Productive technologies such as the smelting of metal, the creation of ceramics and glass, involve the transformation of one or more materials into another. What could be more magical than the transformation of sand and ash into a transparent solid material, which can be manipulated into myriad shapes by heating, or given wonderful colours by the addition of particular 'medicines'? We call the product glass, but to earlier generations it would have appeared to be a magical material. Such considerations lead inexorably to the consideration of alchemy.

Change in technologies or the maintenance of existing traditions derive from the complex interaction of the geographical and temporal orders discussed above, plus the shifting nature of the cultural logics through which cause and effect are understood. These are complex factors individually, and even more so in combination, leaving little possibility for an understanding of the history of technology in a linear or progressive manner.

In the ensuing volumes we hope to explore a wide range of technologies and materials, together with a consideration of the richness of relations within which the associated processes of making and using are entwined and woven into the fabric of society. We hope that these volumes will provide a considerable amount of new information, but also new thoughts on how we think about the issue of technology and technological change across the full span of human history.

Many technologies, maybe even most, are a means of connecting with the sacred or harnessing spiritual powers in the process of production. For the Greeks the movement of the sun, moon and stars was important in an understanding of human well-being and destinies. For African iron smiths it was important to reach the correct state of physical and metaphysical purity through abstaining from sex, food and other activities prior to working metals. The most sophisticated products of Bronze Age China were a series of bronze vessels used for celebrating the ancestors and other powers, who, when suitably pleased and honoured, would ensure the health and prosperity of their living descendants. Rather than a Three Age system of stone, bronze and iron, where it was assumed that each material was functionally superior to the previous in helping people to more efficient forms of agriculture and craft production, we can glimpse a more holistic history in which people wrestled with the nature of the universe and their position within it, producing in the process their own forms of subjectivity and feeling of and for the world. For worlds such as the European Bronze Age where perfectly functional swords were thrown into rivers, perhaps as gifts to spiritual powers, or axes placed on hilltops near springs, we need different histories. Such histories will not be based around ages and stages through which any one part of the world inexorably passes, still less all parts.

In order to feed and clothe themselves people develop a broad reservoir of skills and materials from which they can draw and into which they contribute innovations, large and small. People do not live by bread alone, and food, clothing and shelter are, in most times and places, developed within a suite of existential needs and phenomenological demands. Local cultural commons attempt, with varying degrees of success, to support a cultural whole. This rather utopian notion of human history is, of course, continuously deformed by the needs of power. Having implied that the history of technology should not be written around the finest of products deriving from the most skilled techniques, we can see that this becomes less compelling as soon as some have more power than others. Building the first temples and palaces, around 3800 BCE in Mesopotamia, not only created buildings of unprecedented scale and sophistication but also created a demand for many fine things to furnish them and reinforce their power. The Mesopotamian cities witnessed a great burst of innovation, from pots turned on a fast wheel, to filigree and granulation in metalwork and combinations of fine materials drawn from distant sources in quite a new manner. Some craft labour was supported by the city it seems, although how close to slavery some of these craftspersons may have been is subject to further research – Zaccagnini (1983) suggests that at Mari at least this was limited to weavers. Once again the power of the leader derived from their special relationship with the gods, or in Egypt from the fact that the pharaoh was a god. What we see as the political and economic basis of power, which organized and centralized surplus food production, mined and traded for materials and forced craft workers into novelty, was again wrapped round with issues of the sacred. Inside the enormous spaces of the temples, probably hung round with textiles and floored with carpets, sat the hungry gods, in the form of their statues, who needed regular care and periodic outings on land or water on sacred days, whose dates were partly determined by the movements of bodies in the sky. The history of pottery or bronze making does not exist divorced from the mixed divine and human powers of the world, nor is technology a separate subsystem causing changes in other aspects of life.

Technology, if we can designate and delimit such a thing at all, is a total social fact. If we follow the thread that we call bronze working, it can take us variously to the history of axes, chisels and awls, joining with that of wood, trees and forestry, to the history of swords, halberds and daggers and so into notions of combat and self-definition through fighting, or food and drink in the form of cauldrons, bowls or massive Chinese bronzes. The same is true of histories of textile making, pottery production or the growing and cooking of food. Our necessary specialisms in the present often cause us to think about and analyse one set of materials, so that the pottery specialist lives in a slightly separate world to the ancient metallurgist. But such present day divisions should not lead us to think that our favourite material existed in a world of its own in the past, nor that purely pragmatic considerations were often (ever?) important to people of the ancient worlds we study.

The reservoir of shared materials and skills in the past spilled across materials and contexts, so that pyrotechnology, for instance, was important to many alterations of materials, and an innovation in the firing of pots might well provide inspiration for those working copper or bronze (if they were not the same people). Just as the past exists as a whole, so should our understanding of it in the present. The wealth of specialisms within archaeology are absolutely necessary, but so is the need to weave reasonably whole cloth out of individual threads. A commitment to a rounded past also embeds what we might call technology into what we call the sacred, so that the divisions we might now make between the sacred and the practical did not exist in many past societies. The prospect of producing a whole out of our analytical parts is a daunting one, but, unless we attempt to sketch the rounded nature of human life and the non-linear complexities of its histories, the past will remain a series of fragments and our attempt to understand human diversity and difference will end in failure.

References

Abram, D. (1996). *The Spell of the Sensuous: Perception and Language in a More-than-Human World*. New York: Pantheon Books.

Agamben, G. (2004). *The Open: Man and Animal*. Stanford: Stanford University Press.

Barabási, A.-L. (2002). *Linked: The New Science of Networks*. Cambridge, MA: Pegasus.

Barabási, A.-L. and Albert, R. (1999). Emergence of scaling in random networks. *Science*, **286**, 509–12.

Barker, G. (2006). *The Agricultural Revolution in Prehistory: Why Did Foragers Become Farmers?* Oxford: Oxford University Press.

Bender Jørgensen, L., Sofaer, J. and Sørensen, M. L. S. (2018). *Creativity in the Bronze Age*. Cambridge: Cambridge University Press.

Bentley, R. A. and Maschner, H. D. G. (2001). Stylistic change as a self-organized critical phenomenon: An archaeological study in complexity. *Journal of Archaeological Method and Theory*, **8**, 35–66.

Bentley, R. A. and Shennan, S. J. (2003). Cultural transmission and stochastic network growth. *American Antiquity*, **68**, 459–85.

Bick, M. J. A. (1963). 'Diffusion of innovations' Everett M. Rogers. *American Anthropologist*, **65**, 1146–7.

Binford, S. and Binford, L. (1968). *New Perspectives in Archaeology*. Chicago: Aldine Press.

Bostock, J. and Riley, T. (1855–57). *The Natural History of Pliny*, 6 Vols. London: Henry G. Bohn.

Bourdieu, P. (1990). *The Logic of Practice*. Stanford: Stanford University Press.

Bray, P., Cuénod, A., Gosden, C. et al. (2015). Form and flow: The 'karmic cycle' of copper. *Journal of Archaeological Science*, **56**, 202–9.

Bray, P., Sainsbury, V. and Pollard, A. M. (in press). The significance of antimony patterns in 1st millennium A.D. European and Near Eastern copper-alloy and glass: Parallel or overlapping stories?

Brysbaert, A. (2007). Cross-craft and cross-cultural interactions during the Aegean and Eastern Mediterranean Late Bronze Age. In S. Antoniadou and A. Pace, eds., *Mediterranean Crossroads*, pp. 325–59. Athens: Pierides Foundation.

Brysbaert, A. (2011). Technologies of re-using and recycling in the Aegean and beyond. In A. Brysbaert, ed., *Tracing Prehistoric Social Networks through Technology: A Diachronic Perspective on the Aegean*, pp. 183–203. New York: Routledge.

Brysbaert, A. and Gorgues, A. (eds.) (2017). *Artisans versus Nobility? Multiple Identities of Elites and 'Commoners' Viewed through the Lens of Crafting from the Chalcolithic to the Iron Ages in Europe and the Mediterranean.* Leiden: Sidestone Press.

Burford, A. (1972). *Craftsmen in Greek and Roman Society.* Ithaca: Cornell University Press.

Burke, R. B. (trans.) (1928). *Opus Majus, Roger Bacon*, 2 Vols. Philadelphia: University of Pennsylvania Press.

Campion, N. (2009). *A History of Western Astrology*, Vol. 2: *The Medieval and Modern Worlds.* London: Bloomsbury.

Chikashige, M. (1976). *Oriental Alchemy.* New York: Samuel Weiser (reprint of *Alchemy and Other Chemical Achievements of the Ancient Orient: The Civilization of Japan and China in Early Times as Seen from the Chemical Point of View.* Rokakuho Uchida, Tokyo, 1936).

Childe, V. G. (1936). *Man Makes Himself.* London: Watts.

Childe, V. G. (1954). Early forms of society. In C. Singer, E. J. Holmyard and A. R. Hall, eds., *A History of Technology*, Vol. 1: *From Early Times to Fall of Ancient Empires*, pp. 38–57. Oxford: Clarendon Press.

Clarke, D. L. (1968). *Analytical Archaeology.* London: Methuen.

Craddock, P. T. (2000a). Historical survey of gold refining: 1 Surface treatments and refining worldwide, and in Europe prior to AD 1500. In A. Ramage and P. T. Craddock, eds., *King Croesus' Gold: Excavations at Sardis and the History of Gold Refining*, pp. 27–53. London: British Museum Press.

Craddock, P. T. (2000b). Historical survey of gold refining: 2 Post-medieval Europe. In A. Ramage and P. T. Craddock, eds., *King Croesus' Gold: Excavations at Sardis and the History of Gold Refining*, pp. 54–71. London: British Museum Press.

Dalley, S. (1984). *Mari and Karana: Two Old Babylonian Cities.* London: Longman.

Danvers, J. (1893). The manufactures of India: Their state and prospects. *Journal of the Society of Arts*, **41**, 602–20.

Darwin, C. (1868). *The Variation of Animals and Plants under Domestication.* New York: O. Judd.

Daumas, M. (1960). L'Histoire Generale des Techniques. *Technology and Culture*, **1**, 415–18.

Daumas, M. (1962). *Histoire Générale des Techniques,* Tome 1: *Les Origines de la Civilisation Technique.* Paris: Presses Universitaires de France.

Daumas, M. (1965). *Histoire Générale des Techniques*, Tome 2: *Les Premieres Etapes Du Machinisme.* Paris: Presses Universitaires de France.

Daumas, M. (1968). *Histoire Générale des Techniques*, Tome 3: *L'expansion Du Machinisme*. Paris: Presses Universitaires de France.

Daumas, M. (1979). *Histoire Générale des Techniques, Tome 4: Les Techniques de la Civilisation Industrielle, Energie et Matériaux*. Paris: Presses Universitaires de France.

Daumas, M. (1998). *Histoire Générale des Techniques, Tome 5: Les Techniques de la Civilisation Industrielle: Transformation, Communication, Facteur Humain*. Paris: Presses Universitaires de France.

De Sola Price, D. (1975). *Gears from the Greeks: The Antikythera Mechanism a Calendar Computer from c. 80 BC*. New York: Science History.

Descola, P. (2013). *Beyond Nature and Culture*. Chicago: Chicago University Press.

Efstathiou, K. and Efstathiou, M. (2018). Celestial gearbox: Oldest known computer is a mechanism designed to calculate the location of the sun, moon, and planets. *Mechanical Engineering*, **140**, 31–5.

Eggenschwiler, C. E. (1932). Effect of antimony on the mechanical properties of a bearing bronze (Cu 80: Sn 10: Pb 10). *Bureau of Standards Journal of Research*, **8**, 625–34.

Elliot Smith, G. (1915). *The Migrations of Early Cultures: A Study of the Significance of the Geographical Distribution of the Practice of Mummification as Evidence of the Migration of Peoples and the Spread of Certain Customs and Beliefs*. Manchester: Manchester University Press (2nd ed. 1929).

Evans, J., Carman, C. C. and Thorndyke, A. (2010). Solar anomaly and planetary displays in the Antikythera mechanism. *Journal for the History of Astronomy*, **41**, 1–39.

Fairbank, J. K. (1971). Review: Clerks and craftsmen in China and the West: Lectures and addresses on the history of science and technology by Joseph Needham. *Technology and Culture*, **12**, 328–31.

Feldhaus, F. M. (1914). *Die Technik der Vorzeit, der geschichtlichen Zeit und der Naturvölker: ein Handbuch für Archäologen und Historiker, Museen und Sammler, Kunsthändler und Antiquare*. Leipzig: Engelmann (reprint 1971).

Feldhaus, F. M. (1928). *Kulturgeschichte der Technik*, 2 Vols. Berlin: Salle (reprint 1980).

Feldhaus, F. M. (1931). *Die Technik der Antike und des Mittelalters*. Potsdam: Akademische Verlagsgesellschaft Athenaion (reprint 1971).

Finlay, R. (2000). China, the West, and world history in Joseph Needham's science and civilisation in China. *Journal of World History*, **11**, 265–303.

Flannery, K. V. (1972). The cultural evolution of civilizations. *Annual Review of Ecology and Systematics*, **3**, 399–426.

Forbes, R. J. (1940–1950). *Bibliographia Antiqua: Philosophia naturalis-A. D.1939 Nos. 1–10751*, 10 Vols. Leiden: Nederlandsch Instituut voor het Nabije Oosten.

Forbes, R. J. (1955a). *Studies in Ancient Technology*, Vol. 1: *Bitumen and Petroleum in Antiquity; The Origin of Alchemy; Water Supply*. Leiden: E. J. Brill (2nd ed. 1964, 3rd ed. 1993).

Forbes, R. J. (1955b). *Studies in Ancient Technology*, Vol. 2: *Irrigation and Drainage; Power; Land Transport and Road-Building; The Coming of the Camel*. Leiden: E. J. Brill (2nd rev. ed. 1965, 3rd ed. 1993).

Forbes, R. J. (1955c). *Studies in Ancient Technology*, Vol. 3: *Cosmetics and Perfumes in Antiquity; Food, Alcoholic Beverages, Vinegar; Food in Classical Antiquity: Fermented Beverages 500 B.C.–1500 A.D.; Crushing; Salts, Preservation Processes, Mummification; Paints, Pigments, Inks and Varnishes*. Leiden: E. J. Brill (2nd ed. 1965, 3rd ed. 1993).

Forbes, R. J. (1956). *Studies in Ancient Technology*, Vol. 4: *The Fibres and Fabrics of Antiquity; Washing, Bleaching, Fulling and Felting; Dyes and Dyeing; Spinning; Sewing, Basketry and Weaving and Looms: Fabrics and Weavers*. Leiden: E. J. Brill (reprint 1964, 2nd rev. ed. 1964, reprint 1987).

Forbes, R. J. (1957). *Studies in Ancient Technology*, Vol. 5: *Leather in Antiquity; Sugar and Its Substitutes in Antiquity; Glass*. Leiden: E. J. Brill (2nd rev. ed. 1966).

Forbes, R. J. (1958). *Studies in Ancient Technology*, Vol. 6: *Heat and Heating; Refrigeration, the Art of Cooling and Producing Cold; Light*. Leiden: E. J. Brill (2nd rev. ed. 1966).

Forbes, R. J. (1963). *Studies in Ancient Technology*, Vol. 7: *Ancient Geology; Ancient Mining and Quarrying; Ancient Mining Techniques*. Leiden: E. J. Brill (2nd rev. ed. 1966).

Forbes, R. J. (1964a). *Studies in Ancient Technology*, Vol. 8: *Metallurgy in Antiquity, Part 1: Early Metallurgy, the Smith and His Tools, Gold, Silver and Lead, Zinc and Brass*. Leiden: E. J. Brill (2nd rev. ed. 1971).

Forbes, R. J. (1964b). *Studies in Ancient Technology*, Vol. 9: *Metallurgy in Antiquity, Part 2: Copper and Bronze, Tin, Arsenic, Antimony and Iron*. Leiden: E. J. Brill (2nd rev. ed. 1972).

Fox, C. (1958). *Pattern and Purpose: Early Celtic Art in Britain*. Cardiff: Museum of Wales.

Freeth, T., Bitsakis, Y., Moussas, X. et al. (2006). Decoding the ancient Greek astronomical calculator known as the Antikythera mechanism. *Nature*, **444**, 587–91.

Freeth, T., Higgon, D., Dacanalis, A. et al. (2021). A model of the cosmos in the ancient Greek Antikythera mechanism. *Scientific Reports*, **11**, 5821.

Gandon, E. (2011). *Influence of Cultural Constraints in the Organization of the Human Movement: Proposition of a Theoretical Framework and Empirical Support through the Example of Pottery-Throwing (France/India Prajapati/ India Multani Khumar)*. PhD Thesis, Marseille University.

Gell, A. (1998). *Art and Agency: An Anthropological Theory*. Oxford: Clarendon Press.

Georgakopoulou, M., Bassiakos, Y. and Philaniotou, O. (2011). Seriphos surfaces: A study of copper slag heaps and copper sources in the context of early Bronze Age Aegean metal production. *Archaeometry*, **53**, 123–45.

Gladstone, J. H. (1892). On metallic copper, tin and antimony from ancient Egypt. *Proceedings of the Society of Biblical Archaeology*, **14**, 223–8.

Gosden, C. (2020). *The History of Magic: From Alchemy to Witchcraft, from the Ice Age to the Present*. London: Viking.

Gosden, C. and Malafouris, L. (2015). Process archaeology (P-Arch). *World Archaeology*, **47**, 701–17.

Guzman, G. G. (2010). European captives and craftsmen among the Mongols, 1231–1255. *The Historian*, **72**, 122–50.

Hackett, E. J. (2008). *The Handbook of Science and Technology Studies*, 3rd ed. Cambridge, MA: MIT Press and Society for Social Studies of Science.

Haraway, D. (1991). *Simians, Cyborgs, and Women: The Reinvention of Nature*. Abingdon: Routledge.

Harvey, G. (2005). *Animism: Respecting the Living World*. London: Hurst.

Hawthorne, J. G. and Smith, C. S. (1963). *On Divers Arts: The Treatise of Theophilus*. Chicago: Chicago University Press.

Heidegger, M. (1977). *The Question Concerning Technology and Other Essays*. New York: Harper Perennial.

Hennessy, E. B. (1969a). *A History of Technology & Invention: Progress through the Ages,* Vol. 1: *The Origins of Technological Civilization*. New York: Crown.

Hennessy, E. B. (1969b). *A History of Technology & Invention: Progress through the Ages,* Vol. 2: *The First Stages of Mechanization*. New York: Crown.

Henrich, J. (2004). Demography and cultural evolution: How adaptive cultural processes can produce maladaptive losses – the Tasmanian case. *American Antiquity*, **69**, 197–214.

Hodder, I. (2013). *Entangled: An Archaeology of the Relationship between Humans and Things*. Oxford: Wiley-Blackwell.

Holorenshaw, H. (1973). The making of an honorary Taoist. In M. Teich and R. Young, eds., *Changing Perspectives in the History of Science: Essays in Honour of Joseph Needham*, pp. 1–20. London: Heinemann.

Hoover, H. C. and Hoover, L. H. (1912). *Agricola, De Re Metallica*. London: The Mining Magazine (reprint 1950).

Hsia, F. and Schäfer, D. (2019). History of science, technology, and medicine: A second look at Joseph Needham. *Isis*, **110**, 94–9.

Huxham, J. (1756). *Medical and Chemical Observations Upon Antimony*. London: Hinton (reprint from *Philosophical Transactions of the Royal Society*, **48**, 832–69, 1753).

Ingold, T. (2000). *The Perception of the Environment*. London: Routledge.

Ingold, T. (2011). *Being Alive: Essays on Movement, Knowledge and Description*. London: Routledge.

Ingold, T. (2013). *Making: Anthropology, Archaeology, Art and Architecture*. London: Routledge.

Jones, A. (2017). *A Portable Cosmos: Revealing the Antikythera Mechanism, Scientific Wonder of the Ancient World*. Oxford: Oxford University Press.

Kamal, H. (1926). Antimony in ancient Egyptian medicine. *British Medical Journal*, **1926**, 1102.

Killick, D. (2001). Science, speculation and the origins of extractive metallurgy. In D. R. Brothwell and A. M. Pollard, eds., *Handbook of Archaeological Sciences*, pp. 483–92. Chichester: Wiley.

Kim, J. (2001). Elite strategies and the spread of technological innovation: The spread of iron in the Bronze Age societies of Denmark and southern Korea. *Journal of Anthropological Archaeology*, **20**, 442–78.

Kingery, W. D. (1996). A role for materials science. In W. D. Kingery, ed., *Learning from Things*, pp. 175–80. Washington, DC: Smithsonian Institution Press.

Knappett, C. (2006). Beyond skin: Layering and networking in art and archaeology. *Cambridge Archaeological Journal*, **16**, 239–51.

Kranzberg, M. (1960). Charles Singer and *A History of Technology*. *Technology and Culture*, **1**, 299–302.

Kuijpers, M. H. G. (2018). *An Archaeology of Skill: Metalworking Skill and Material Specialization in Early Bronze Age Central Europe*. London: Routledge.

Kuzmin, Y. V. (2006). Chronology of the earliest pottery in East Asia: Progress and pitfalls. *Antiquity*, **80**, 362–71.

Kuzmin, Y. V. (2013). Origin of old world pottery as viewed from the early 2010s: When, where and why? *World Archaeology*, **45**, 539–56.

Latour, B. (1993). *We Have Never Been Modern*. London: Harvester Wheatsheaf.

Latour, B. (2005). *Re-assembling the Social: An Introduction to Actor Network Theory*. Oxford: Oxford University Press.

Lechtman, H. (1977). Style in technology: Some early thoughts. In H. Lechtman and R. S. Merrill, eds., *Material Culture: Styles, Organization and Dynamics of Technology*, pp. 3–20. St. Paul: West.

Leiss, W. (1972). *The Domination of Nature*. New York: George Braziller.

Lemonnier, P. (1986). The study of material culture today: Towards an anthropology of technical systems. *Journal of Anthropological Archaeology*, **5**, 147–86.

Leroi-Gourhan, A. (1964). *Le geste et la parole I: techniques et langage*. Paris: A. Michel.

Leroi-Gourhan, A. (1965). *Le geste et la parole II: la m'moire el les rythmes*. Paris: A. Michel.

Leroi-Gourhan, A. (1993). *Gesture and Speech (Le geste et la parole)*, trans. A. Bostock Berger. Cambridge, MA: MIT Press.

Lévy-Bruhl, L. (1926). *How Natives Think*. London: George Allen and Unwin.

Li, G., Zhang, M. and Cao, T. (eds.) (1982). *Explorations in the History of Science and Technology in China. Compiled in Honour of the Eightieth Birthday of Dr. Joseph Needham FRS, FBA*. Shanghai: Shanghai Chinese Classics Publishing House.

Limet, H. (1960). *Le Travail du Métal au Pays de Sumer au Temps de la IIIe Dynastie d'Ur*. Paris: Les Belles Lettres.

Linden, J. S. (2003). *The Alchemy Reader: From Hermes Trismegistus to Isaac Newton*. Cambridge: Cambridge University Press.

Major, J. S. (1975). Review: Science and civilisation in China, Vol. 5: Chemistry and chemical technology, Part 2: Spagyrical discovery and invention: Magisteries of gold and immortality by Joseph Needham. *Technology and Culture*, **16**, 621–7.

Malafouris, L. (2013). *How Things Shape the Mind: A Theory of Material Engagement*. Boston: MIT Press.

Manitsaris, S., Glushkova, A., Bevilacqua, F. and Moutarde, F. (2014). Capture, modelling and recognition of expert technical gestures in wheel-throwing art of pottery. *ACM Journal on Computing and Cultural Heritage*, **7**(2), 1–15.

Martinón-Torres, M. (2011). Some recent developments in the historiography of alchemy. *Ambix*, **58**, 215–37.

Marx, K. (1867). *Das Kapital, Buch 1: Kritik der politischen Oekonomie*. Hamburg: Otto Meissner.

Matin, M. and Pollard, M. (2015). Historical accounts of cobalt ore processing from the Kashan mine, Iran. *Iran*, **53**, 171–83.

Mauss, M. (1979). *Sociology and Psychology: Essays*. London: Routledge and Kegan Paul.

Mauss, M. (2006). *Techniques, Technology and Civilisation*. Oxford: Berghahn.

McGovern, P. E. (1989). Ceramics and craft interaction: A theoretical framework, with prefatory remarks. In P. E. McGovern, M. D. Notis and W. D. Kingery, eds., *Ceramics and Civilization*, Vol. 4: *Cross-Craft and Cross-Cultural Interactions in Ceramics*, pp. 1–11. Westerville: American Ceramic Society.

Moorey, P. R. S. (1994). *Ancient Mesopotamian Materials and Industries: The Archaeological Evidence*. Oxford: Clarendon Press (reprint 1999).

Morgan, L. H. (1877). *Ancient Society, or Researches in the Lines of Human Progress from Savagery through Barbarism to Civilization*. Chicago: Charles H. Kerr.

Morris, I. (2010). *Why the West Rules – For Now: The Patterns of History, and What They Reveal about the Future*. London: Profile Books.

Mumford, L. (1960). Tools and the man. *Technology and Culture*, **1**, 320–34.

Nakassis, D. (2013). Smiths and herders. In D. Nakassis, ed., *Individuals and Society in Mycenaean Pylos*, pp. 73–116. Leiden: Brill.

Needham, J. (1960). The past in China's present: A cultural, social, and philosophical background for contemporary China. *The Centennial Review of Arts & Science*, **4**, 145–78, 281–308.

Needham, J. (1971). *The Refiner's Fire: The Enigma of Alchemy in East and West*. London: Ruddock.

Needham, J. (1981). *Science in Traditional China: A Comparative Perspective*. Cambridge, MA: Harvard University Press.

Needham, J. and Lu, G,-D (1974). *Science and Civilisation in China*, Vol. 5: *Chemistry and Chemical Technology*, Part 2: *Spagyrical Discovery and Invention: Magisteries of Gold and Immortality*. Cambridge: Cambridge University Press.

Needham, J. and Wang, L. (1954). *Science and Civilisation in China*, Vol. 1: *Introductory Orientations*. Cambridge: Cambridge University Press.

Neumann, H. (1987). *Handwerk in Mesopotamien: Untersuchungen zu seiner Organization in der Zeit der III Dynastie von Ur*. Berlin: Akademie-Verlag.

Nunn, J. F. (1996). *Ancient Egyptian Medicine*. London: British Museum Press.

O'Brien, P. (2009). The Needham question updated: An historiographical survey and elaboration. *History of Technology*, **29**, 7–28.

Perdue, P. C. (2006). Review: Joseph Needham's problematic legacy: Science and civilisation in China, volume 7, part 2. *Technology and Culture*, **47**, 175–8.

Pierce, C. S. (1898). Note on the age of Basil Valentine. *Science*, **8**(189), 169–76.

Pollard, A. M. (1988). Alchemy: A history of early technology. *School Science Review*, **70**, 701–12.

Pollard, A. M., Bray, P., Cuénod, A. et al. (2018). *Beyond Provenance: New Approaches to Interpreting the Chemistry of Archaeological Copper Alloys.* Leuven: Leuven University Press.

Pollard, A. M., Heron, C. and Armitage, R. A. (2017). *Archaeological Chemistry.* Cambridge: Royal Society of Chemistry.

Pooley, G. (1693). VI. An account of digging and preparing the lapis calaminaris, in a letter from Mr. Giles Pooley to Sir Robert Southwel President of the R. S. *Philosophical Transactions of the Royal Society*, **17**, 672–7.

Povey, T. (1693). I. The method, manner and order of the transmutation of copper into brass, &c. By Thomas Povey, Esq; brought into the Royal Society, of which he is a fellow. *Philosophical Transactions of the Royal Society*, **17**, 735–6.

Principe, L. M. (2007). *Chymists and Chymistry: Studies in the History of Alchemy and Early Modern Chemistry.* Sagamore Beach: Science History.

Ricci, A. (1931). *The Travels of Marco Polo.* London: Routledge.

Roberts, B. W. and Thornton, C. P. (eds.) (2014). *Archaeometallurgy in Global Perspective: Methods and Syntheses.* New York: Springer.

Roberts, B. W., Thornton, C. P. and Pigott, V. C. (2009). Development of metallurgy in Eurasia. *Antiquity*, **83**, 1012–22.

Rochberg, F. (2016). *Before Nature: Cuneiform Knowledge and the History of Science.* Chicago: University of Chicago Press.

Rogers, E. M. (2003). *Diffusion of Innovations*, 5th ed. New York: Free Press.

Ronan, C. A. (1978–1995). *The Shorter Science and Civilisation in China: An Abridgement of Joseph Needham's Original Text*, 5 Vols. Cambridge: Cambridge University Press.

Rowley-Conwy, P. (2007). *From Genesis to Prehistory: The Archaeological Three-Age System and its Contested Reception in Denmark, Britain and Ireland.* Oxford: Oxford University Press.

Said, H. M. (ed.) (1990). *Essays on Science: Felicitation Volume in Honour of Dr Joseph Needham.* Karachi: Hamdard Foundation.

Sayre, E. V. and Smith, R. W. (1961). Compositional categories of ancient glass. *Science*, **133**, 1824–6.

Schlanger, N. (1994). Mindful technology: Unleashing the *Chaîne Opératoire* for an archaeology of the mind. In C. Renfrew and E. B. W. Zubrow, eds., *The Ancient Mind: Elements of Cognitive Archaeology*, pp. 143–51. Cambridge: Cambridge University Press.

Sennett, R. (2009). *The Craftsman.* London: Penguin.

Shott, M. J. (2003). Chaîne opératoire and reduction sequence. *Lithic Technology*, **28**, 95–105.

Sillar, B. and Tite, M. S. (2000). The challenge of 'technological choices' for materials science approaches in archaeology. *Archaeometry*, **42**, 2–20.

Singer, C. (1960). How 'A History of Technology' came into being. *Technology and Culture*, **1**, 302–11.

Singer, C., Holmyard, E. J. and Hall, A. R. (1954). *A History of Technology*, Vol. 1: *From Early Times to Fall of Ancient Empires*. Oxford: Clarendon Press.

Singer, C., Holmyard, E. J., Hall, A. R. and Williams, T. I. (1956). *A History of Technology*, Vol. 2: *The Mediterranean Civilizations and the Middle Ages, c.700 B.C. to A.D. 1500*. Oxford: Clarendon Press.

Singer, C., Holmyard, E. J., Hall, A. R. and Williams, T. I. (1957). *A History of Technology*, Vol. 3: *From the Renaissance to the Industrial Revolution, c.1500–c.1750*. Oxford: Clarendon Press.

Singer, C., Holmyard, E. J., Hall, A. R. and Williams, T. I. (1958a). *A History of Technology*, Vol. 4: *The Industrial Revolution, c.1750–c.1850*. Oxford: Clarendon Press.

Singer, C., Holmyard, E. J., Hall, A. R. and Williams, T. I. (1958b). *A History of Technology*, Vol. 5: *The late Nineteenth Century, c.1850–c.1900*. Oxford: Clarendon Press.

Sisco, A. G. and Smith, C. S. (1949). *Bergwerck und Probierbüchlien*. New York: American Institute of Mining and Metallurgical Engineers.

Sisco, A. G. and Smith, C. S. (1951). *Lazarus Ercker's Treatise on Ores and Assaying*. Chicago: University of Chicago Press.

Sismondo, S. (2010). *An Introduction to Science and Technology Studies*, 2nd ed. Chichester: Wiley-Blackwell.

Sluiter, I. (2016). Anchoring innovation: A classical research agenda. *European Review*, **25**, 20–38.

Smith, C. S. (1968). Matter versus material: A historical view. *Science*, **162**, 637–44.

Smith, C. S. (1981). *A Search for Structure: Selected Essays on Science, Art and History*. Cambridge, MA: MIT Press.

Smith, C. S. and Gnudi, M. T. (trans.) (1942). *Biringuccio, De la Pirotechnia*. Chicago: Basic Books.

Stengers, I. (2000). *The Invention of Modern Science*. Minneapolis: University of Minnesota Press.

Stockhammer, P. W. and Maran, J. (eds.) (2017). *Appropriating Innovations: Entangled Knowledge in Eurasia 5000–1500 BCE*. Oxford: Oxbow.

Sun, L., Yang, G., Liu, R. et al. (2021). Global circulation of silver between Ming-Qing China and the Americas: Combining historical texts and scientific analyses. *Archaeometry*, **63**, 627–40.

Svorykin, A. A., Cernysev, V. I. and Os'mova, N. I. (1962). *Geschichte der Technik*. Leipzig: VEB Fachbuchverlag.

Teich, M. and Young, R. (eds.) (1973). *Changing Perspectives in the History of Science: Essays in Honour of Joseph Needham.* London: Heinemann.

Thomas, K. (1971). *Religion and the Decline of Magic.* Harmondsworth: Penguin.

Tite, M. S. (1999). Pottery production, distribution, and consumption: The contribution of the physical sciences. *Journal of Archaeological Method and Theory*, **6**, 181–232.

Tylecote, R. F. (1976). *A History of Metallurgy.* London: The Metals Society.

Tylor, E. B. (1871). *Primitive Culture: Researches into the Development of Mythology, Philosophy, Religion, Language, Art, and Custom*, 2 Vols. London: John Murray.

Vandiver, P. B., Soffer, O., Klima, B. and Svoboda, J. (1989). The origins of ceramic technology at Dolni Věstonice, Czechoslovakia. *Science*, **246**, 1002–8.

von Bertalanffy, L. (1968). *General Systems Theory: Foundations, Development, Applications.* New York: George Braziller.

Waite, A. E. (1893). *The Triumphal Chariot of Antimony. By Basilius Valentinus, with the Commentary of Theodore Kenckvingvis ... Being the Latin Version Published at Amsterdam in the Year 1685, Translated into English with a Biographical Preface.* London: J. Elliott.

Watson, B. (1961). *Records of the Grand Historian of China*, 2 Vols. New York: Columbia University Press.

White, L., Jr (1960). Technology in the Middle Ages. *Technology and Culture*, **1**, 339–44.

White, L., Jr and Spence, J. D. (1984). Review: Science in China. *Isis*, **75**, 171–89.

Williams, T. I. (1978). *A History of Technology*, Vol. 6: *The Twentieth Century, c.1900 to c. 1950, Parts I and II.* Oxford: Clarendon Press.

Yonge, C. D. (trans.) (1877). *Cicero's Tusculan Disputations: Also, Treatises on the Nature of the Gods, and on the Commonwealth.* New York: Harper & Brothers.

Zaccagnini, C. (1983). Patterns of mobility among ancient Near Eastern craftsmen. *Journal of Near Eastern Studies*, **42**, 245–64.

Zeder, M. A. (2008). Domestication and early agriculture in the Mediterranean Basin: Origins, diffusion, and impact. *Proceedings of the National Academy of Sciences of the USA*, **105**, 11597–604.

Zvorikine, A. A. (1960). The Soviet history of technology. *Technology and Culture*, **1**, 421–5.

Zvorikine, A. A. (1961). The history of technology as a science and as a branch of learning: A Soviet view. *Technology and Culture*, **2**, 1–4.

Acknowledgements

The contents of this volume represent the culmination of more than ten years of dialogue on this subject by the two authors. It represents the results of many hours of formal and informal discussions with many colleagues and students. We gratefully acknowledge the contribution of Wendy Morrison and Peter Hommel to some of the earlier versions of the text, and particularly to Jianjun Mei, Ann Brysbaert, and Joanna Sofaer who commented on a later version. Any remaining errors, omissions and idiosyncrasies are entirely the responsibility of the authors.

Cambridge Elements ≡

Archaeological Perspectives on Materials and Technologies

A. Mark Pollard
University of Oxford
A. Mark Pollard is Emeritus Professor of Archaeological Science at the University of Oxford. His publications include *Beyond Provenance: New Approaches to Interpreting the Chemistry of Archaeological Copper Alloys* (University of Leuven Press, 2018), *Archaeological Chemistry* (Royal Society of Chemistry, 2017), and *Handbook of Archaeological Sciences* (Wiley, 2001).

Chris Gosden
University of Oxford
Chris Gosden is Professor of European Archaeology at the University of Oxford, and his publications include *Celtic Art in Europe: Making Connections* (2014), *A Technology of Enchantment? Exploring Celtic Art 400 BC – AD 100* (2012) and *Archaeology and Colonialism* (2004).

About the Series
Examining technology on a worldwide basis from the earliest human use of tools to the early modern period, this series focuses on new archaeological findings, and integrates these with historical textual sources where they exist. It considers how things were done, why they were done that way, and how an understanding of the world was generated through making and using materials.

Cambridge Elements ≡

Archaeological Perspectives on Materials and Technologies

Elements in the Series

An Archaeological Perspective on the History of Technology
A. Mark Pollard and Chris Gosden

A full series listing is available at: www.cambridge.org/EAMT

CPSIA information can be obtained
at www.ICGtesting.com
Printed in the USA
BVHW041758160223
658686BV00012B/290

This volume represents an introduction to a new worldwide attempt to review the history of technology, which is one of the few since the pioneering publications of the 1960s. It takes an explicit archaeological focus to the study of the history of technology and adopts a more explicit socially embedded view of technology than has commonly been the case in mainstream histories of technology. In doing so, it attempts to introduce a more radical element to explanations of technological change, involving magic, alchemy, animism – in other words, attempting to consider technological change in terms of the 'world view' of those involved in such change rather than from an exclusively Western scientific perspective.

About the series
Examining technology on a worldwide basis from the earliest human use of tools to the early modern period, this series focuses on new archaeological findings, and integrates these with historical textual sources where they exist. It considers how things were done, why they were done that way, and how an understanding of the world was generated through making and using materials.

Series editors
A. Mark Pollard
University of Oxford

Chris Gosden
University of Oxford

Cover image: The Metropolitan Museum of Art, New York, www.metmuseum. org. Purchase, Arthur Ochs Sulzberger and Friends of Arms and Armor Gifts, Arthur Ochs Sulzberger Bequest, and funds from various donors, 2018 (detail)

CAMBRIDGE
UNIVERSITY PRESS

ISBN 978-1-009-18421-2

9 781009 184212 >